I0488043

ZAGREB

SKETCHED

ROBERT ORNIG

Copyright © 2019 by Robert Ornig
All rights reserved. This book or any
portion thereof
may not be reproduced or used in any
manner whatsoever
without the express written permission of
the publisher
except for the use of brief quotations in
a book review.
Printed in the United States of America

DAVID HOCKNEY

Drawing makes you see things clearer, and clearer and clearer still, until your eyes ache.

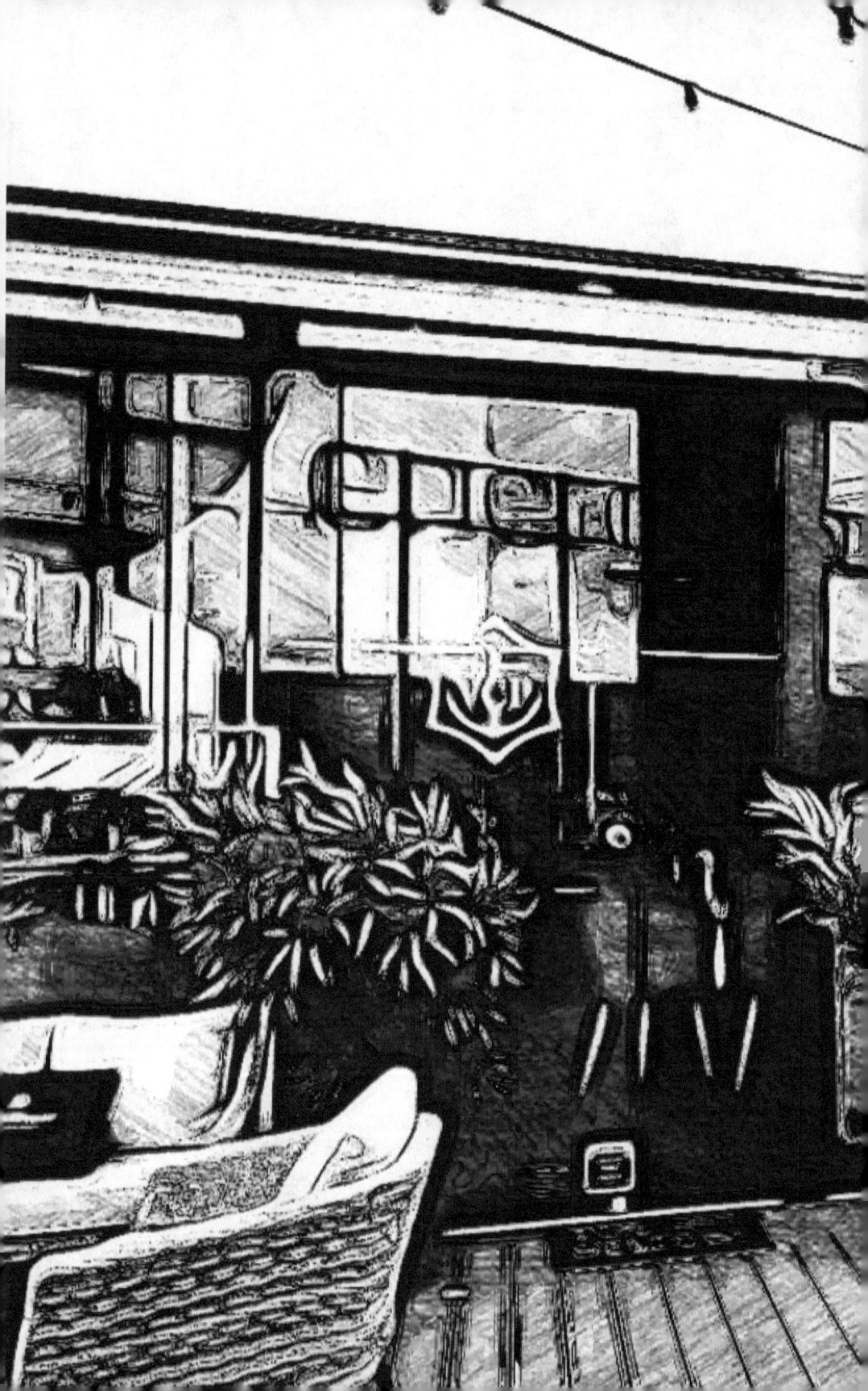

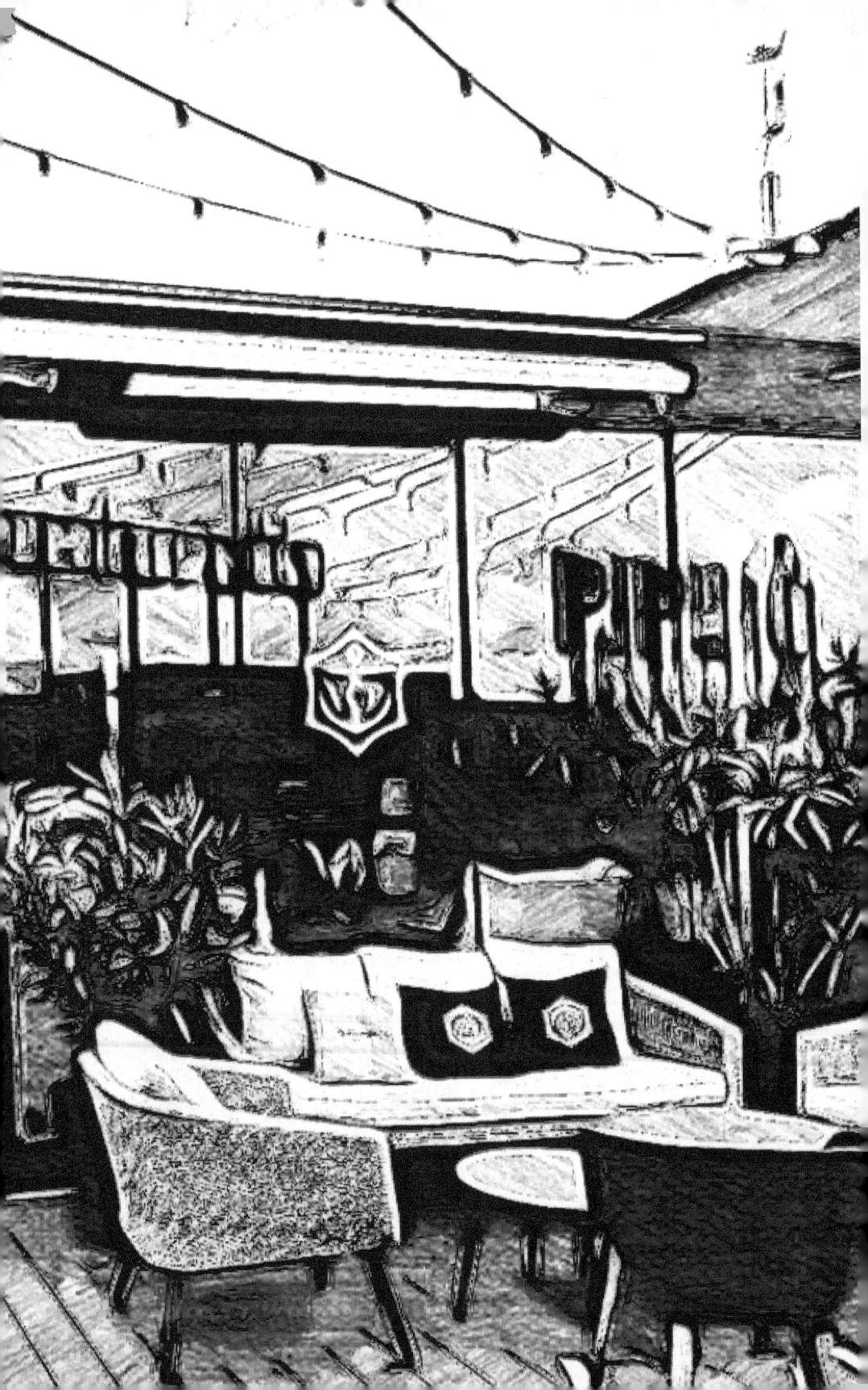

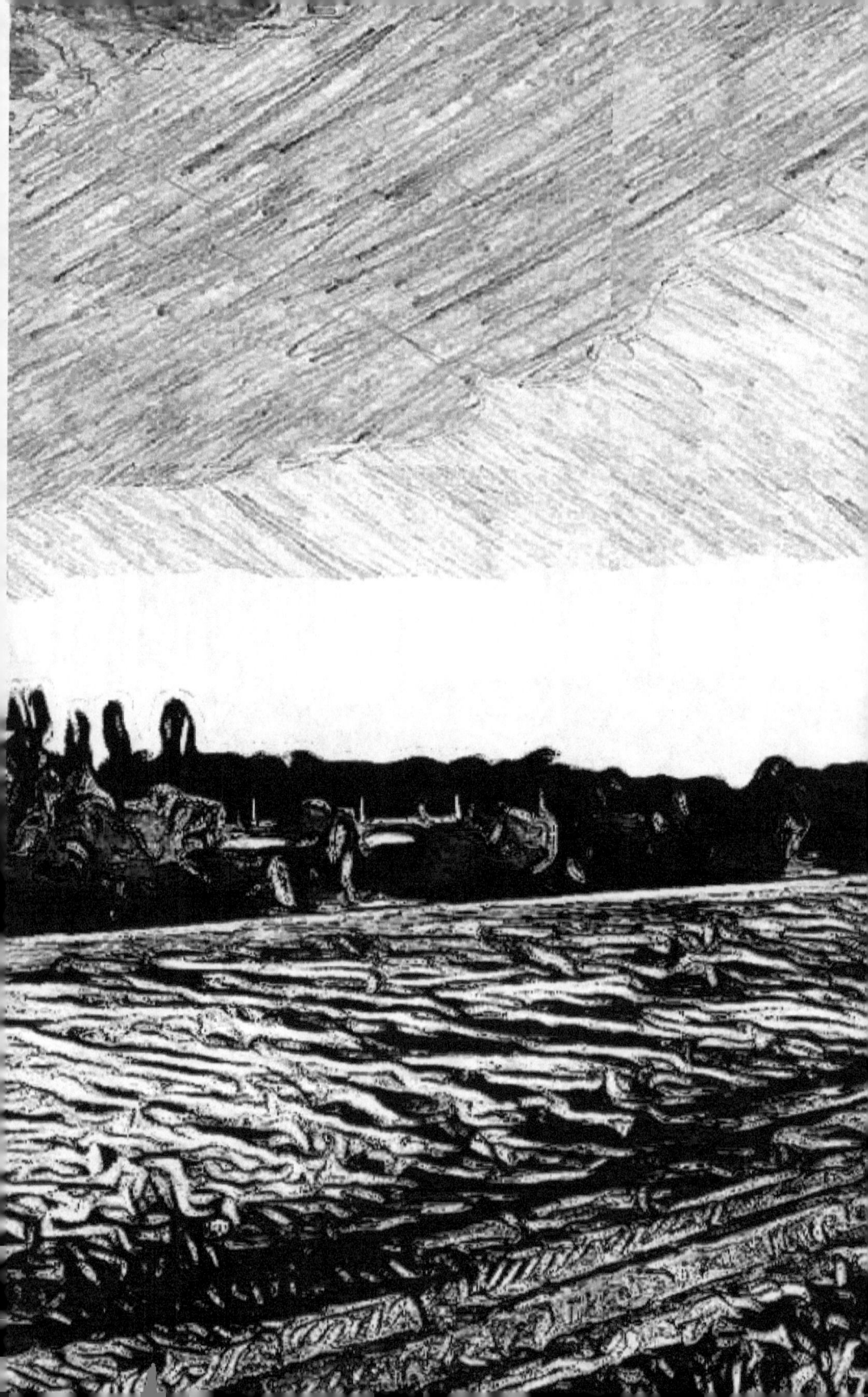

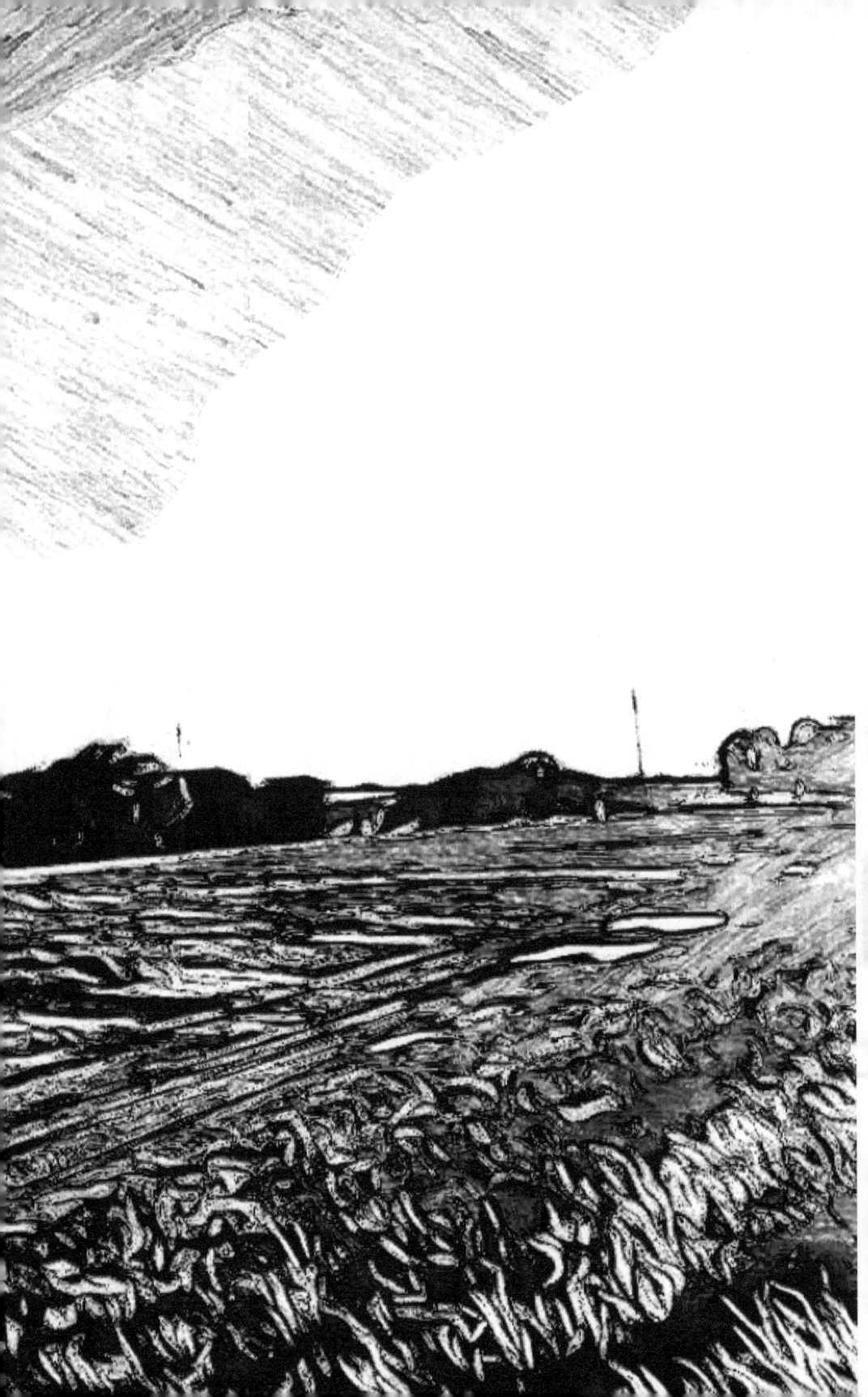

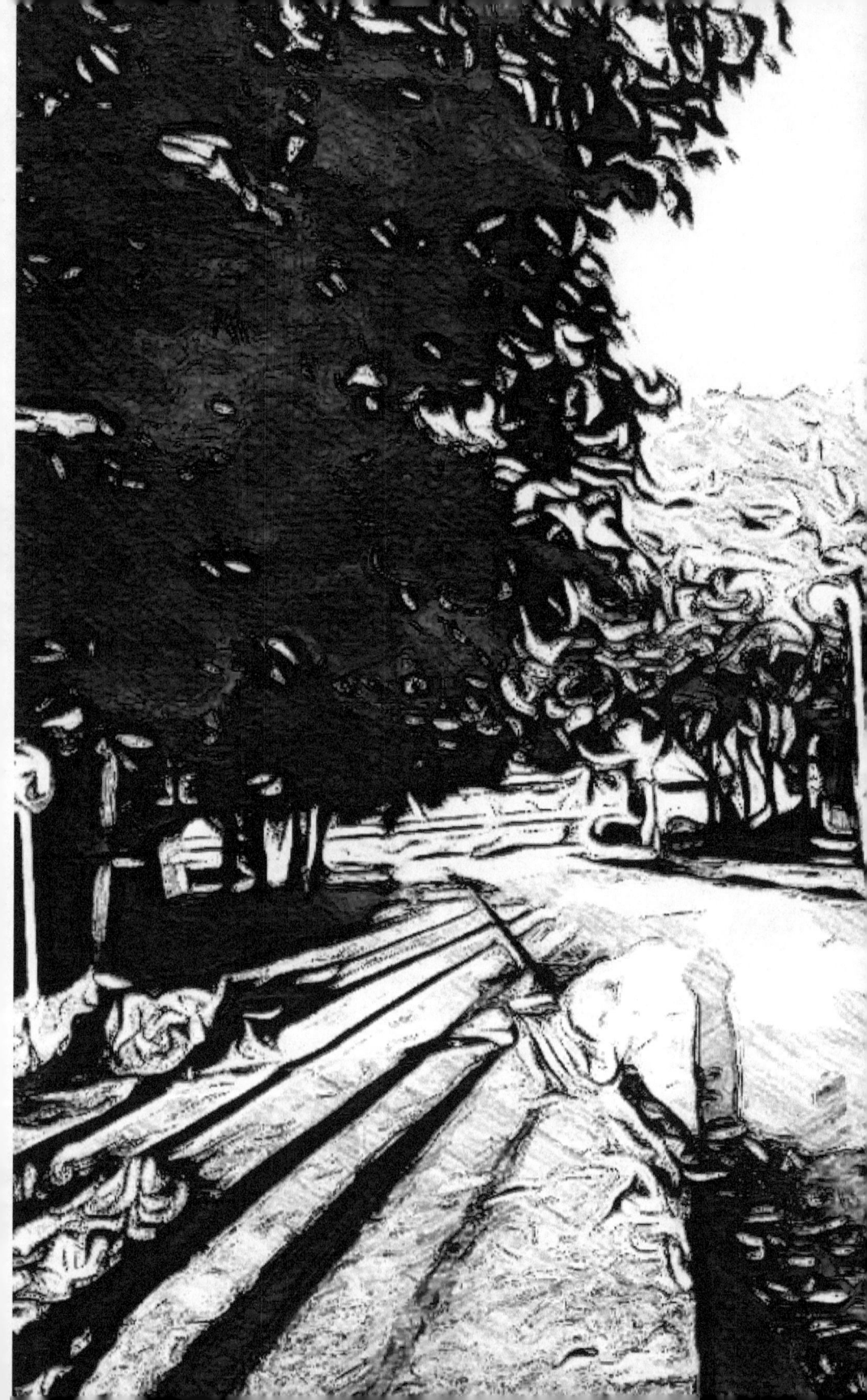

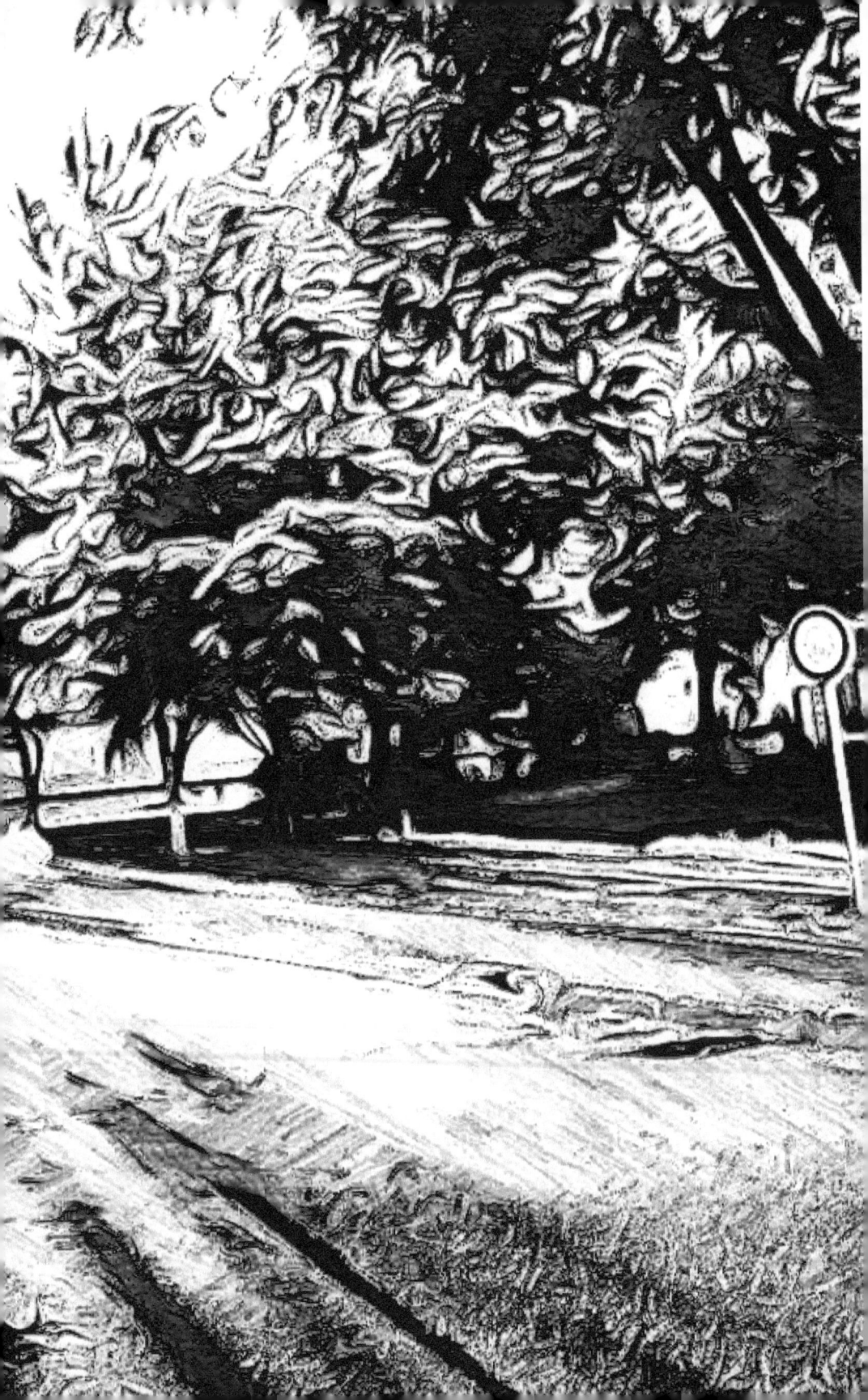

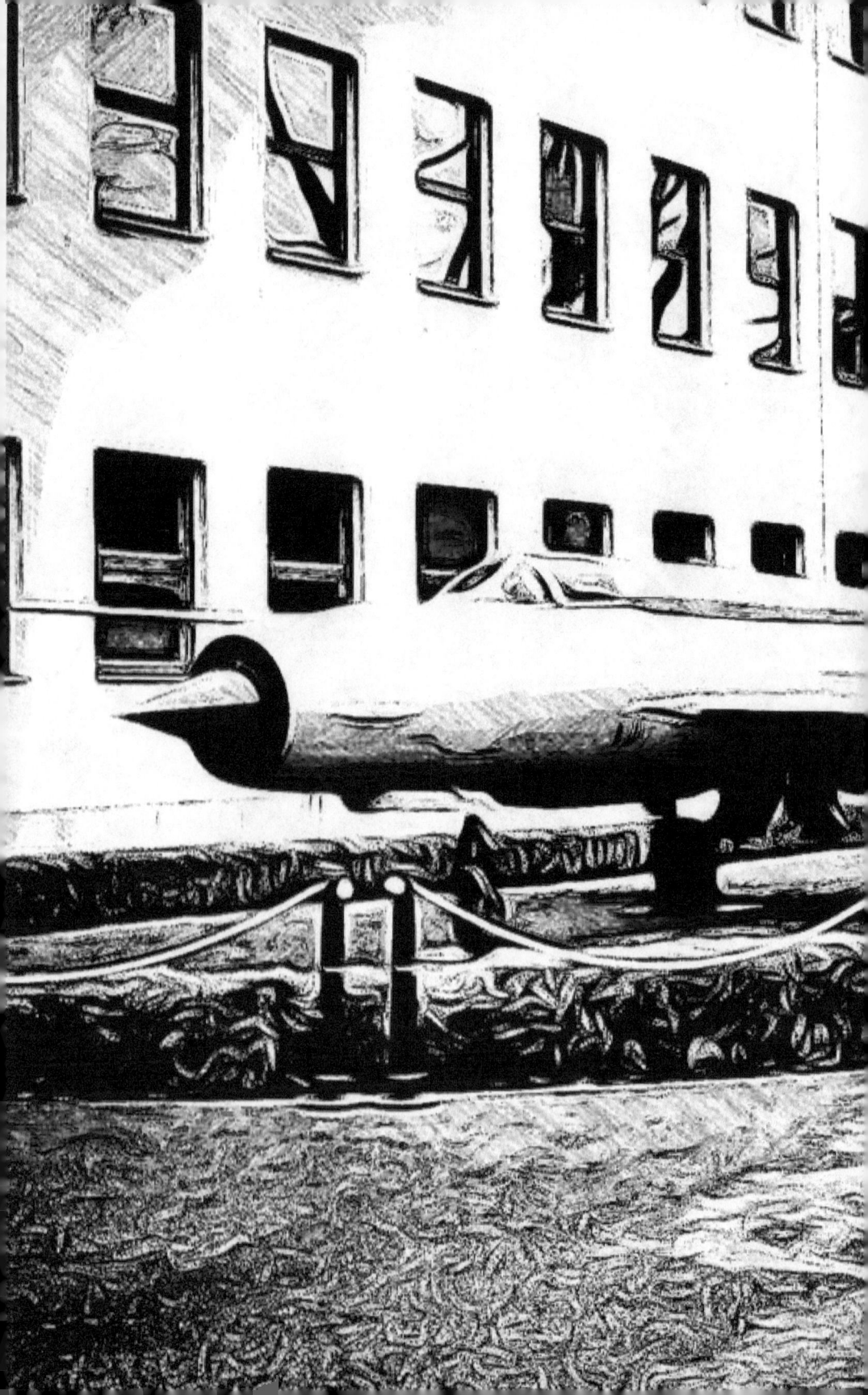

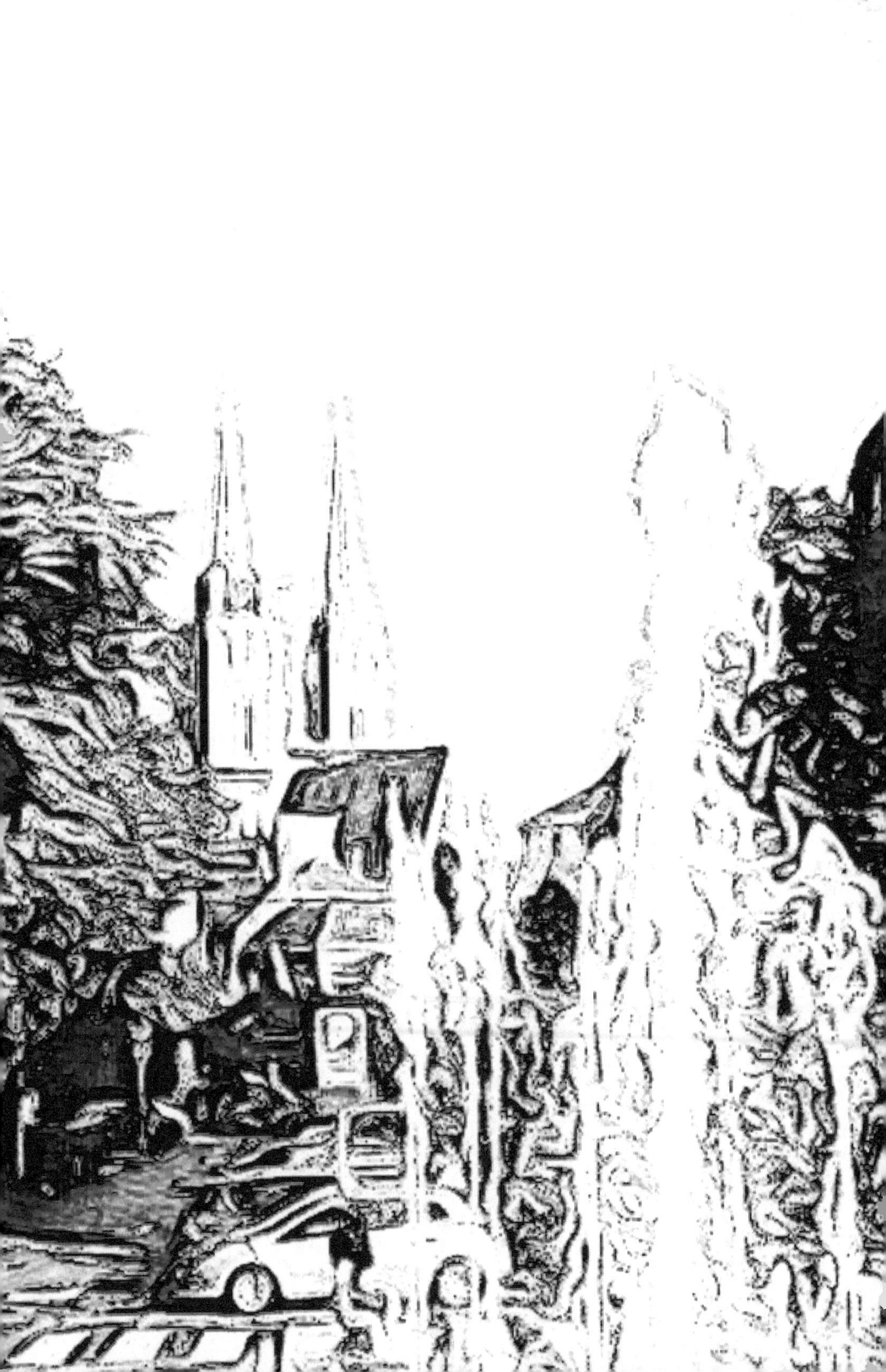

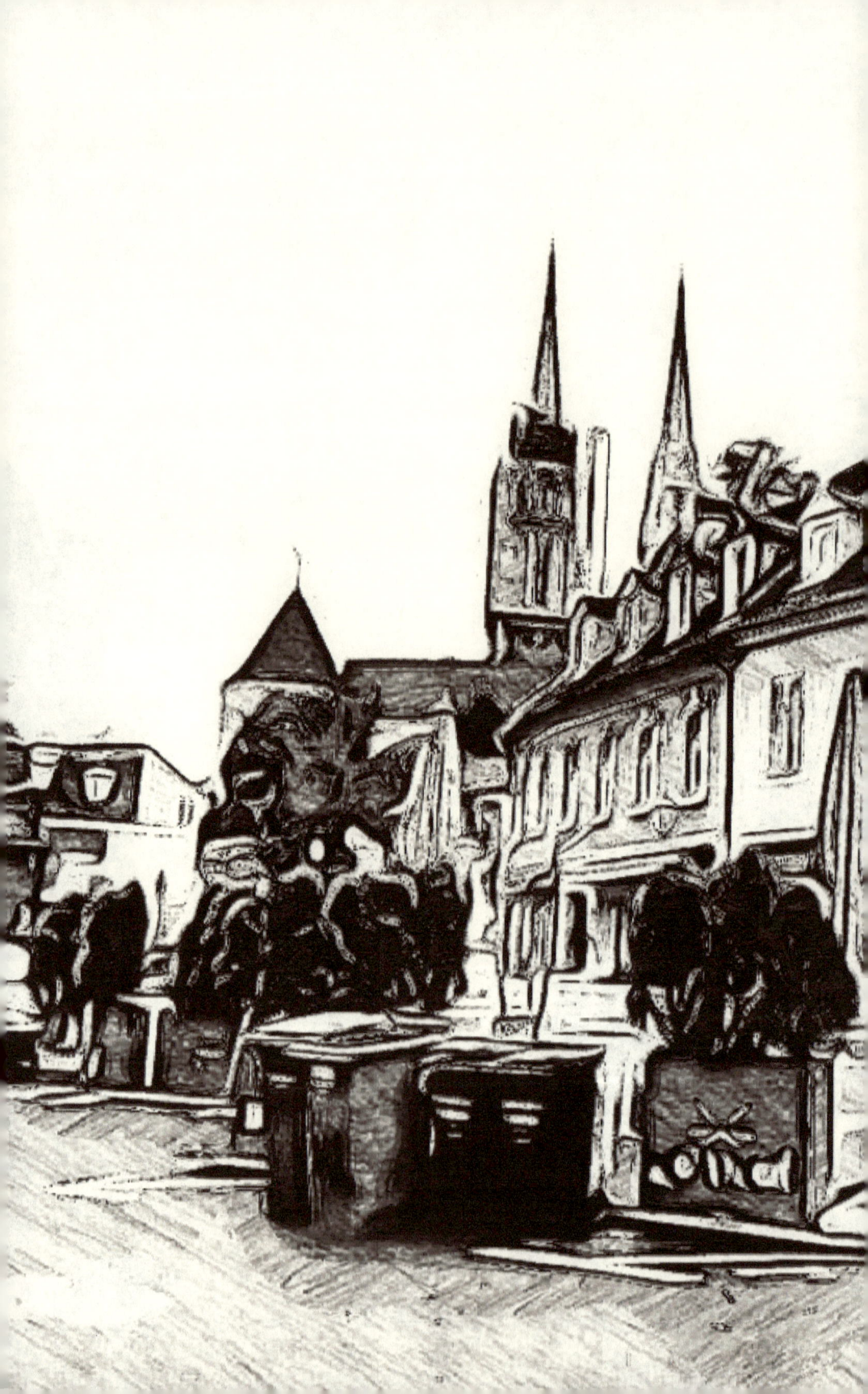

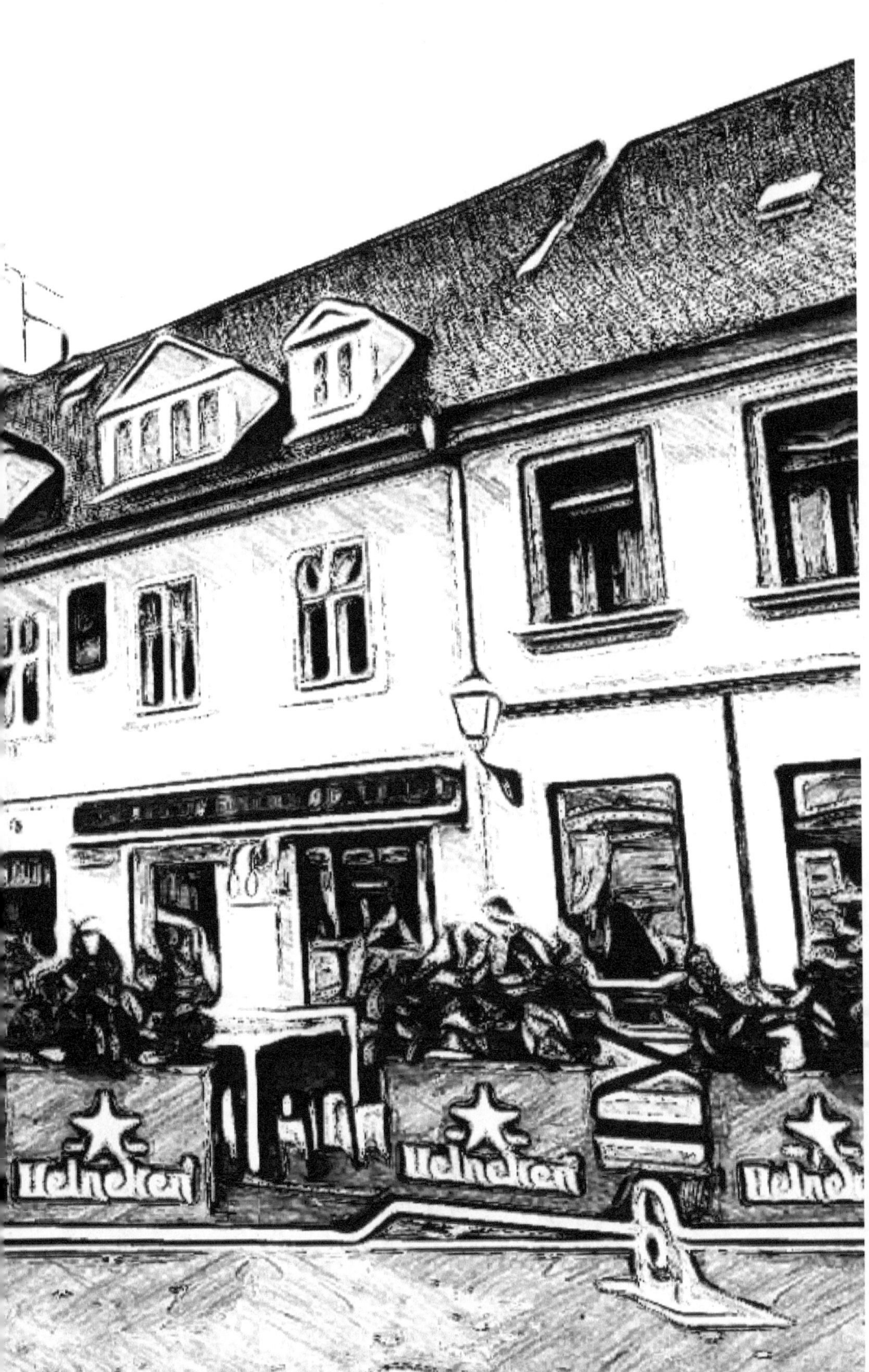

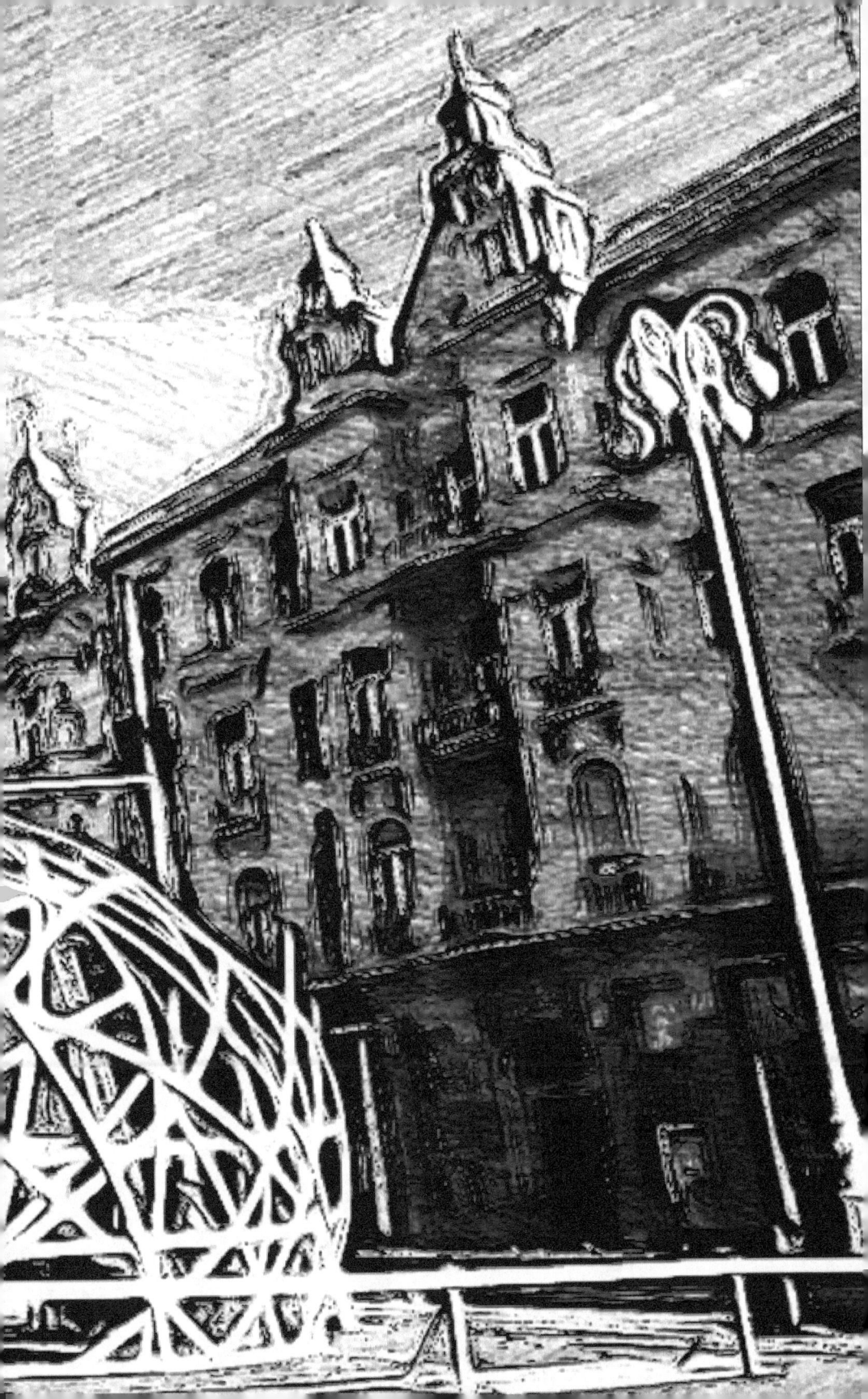

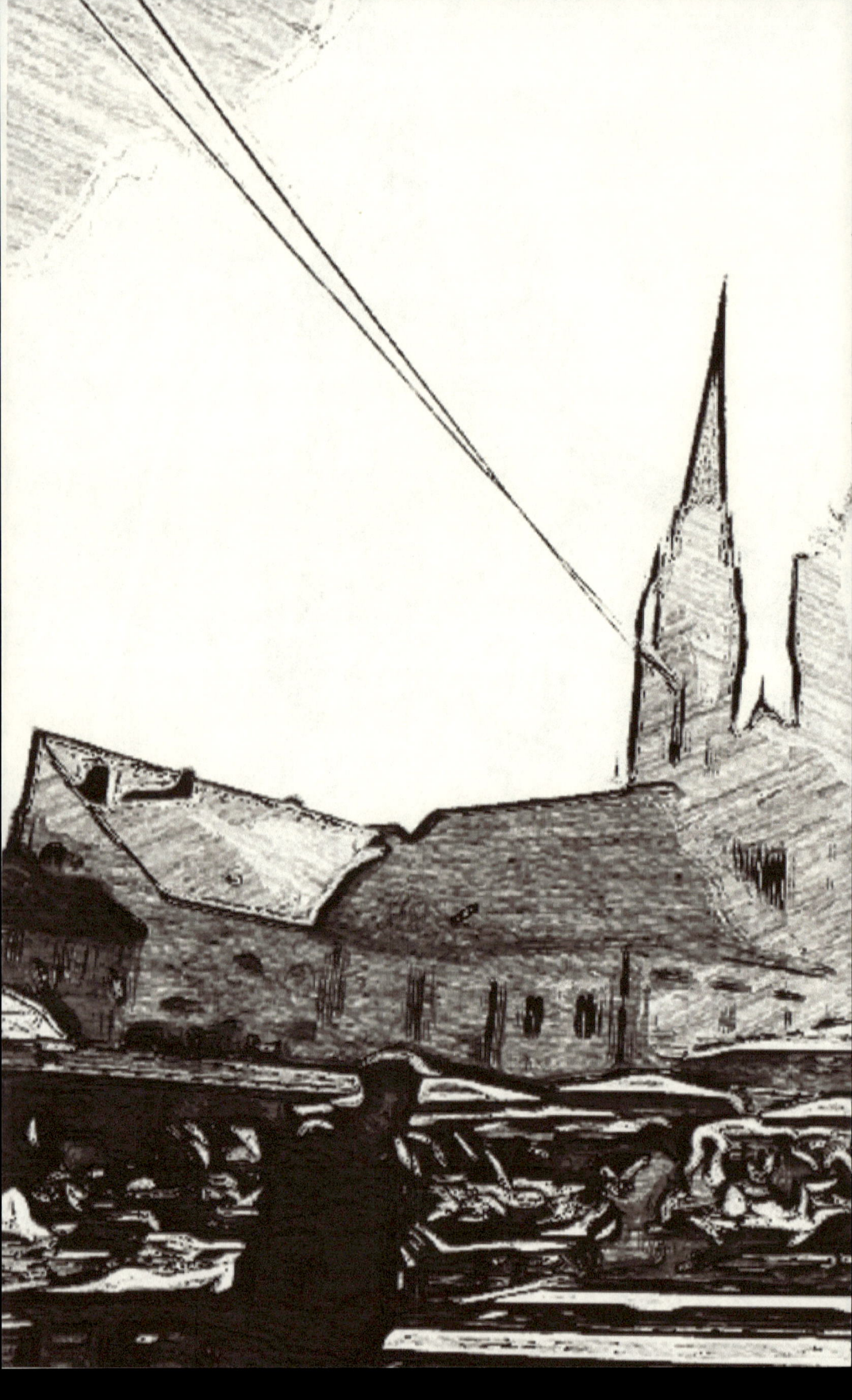

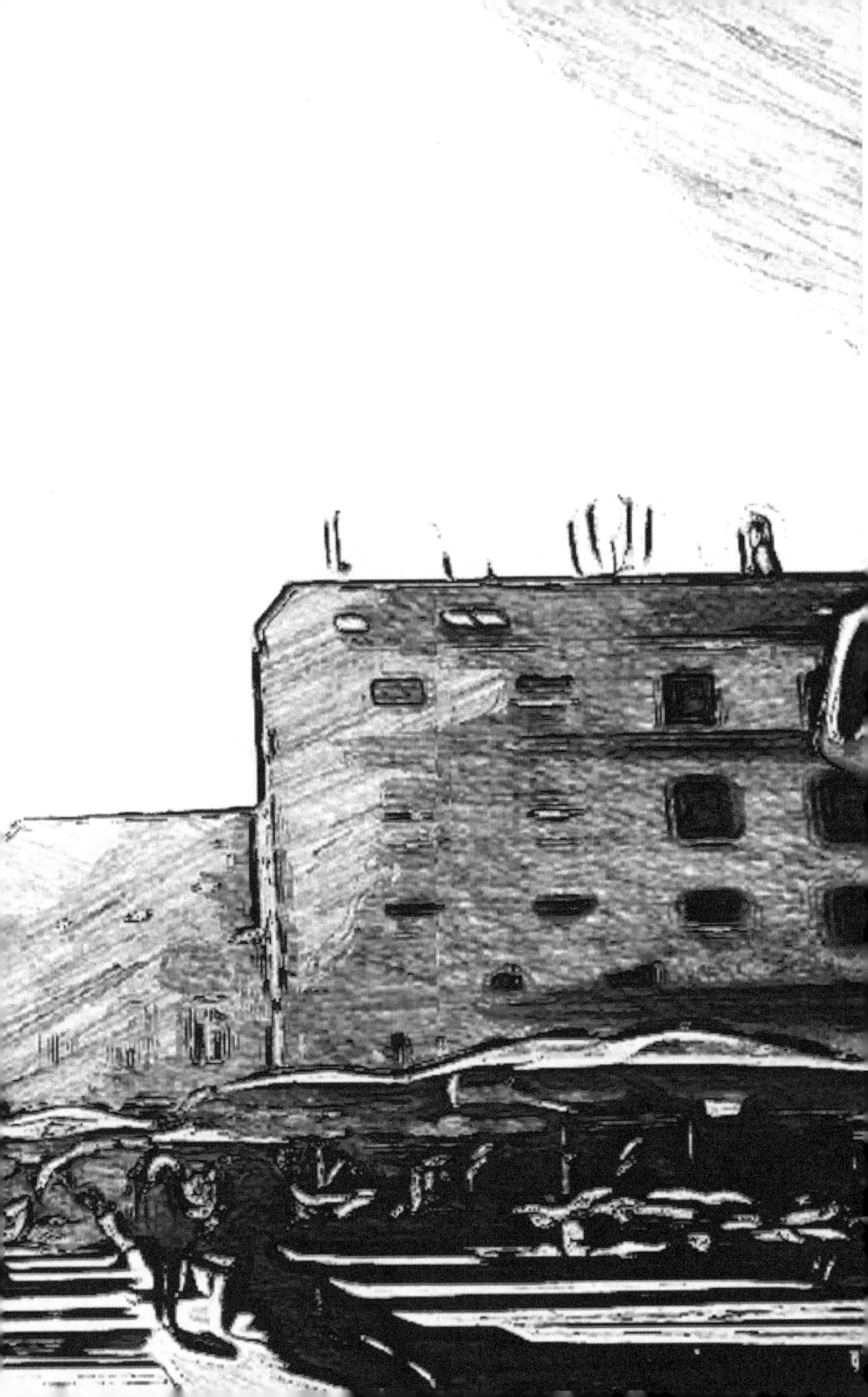

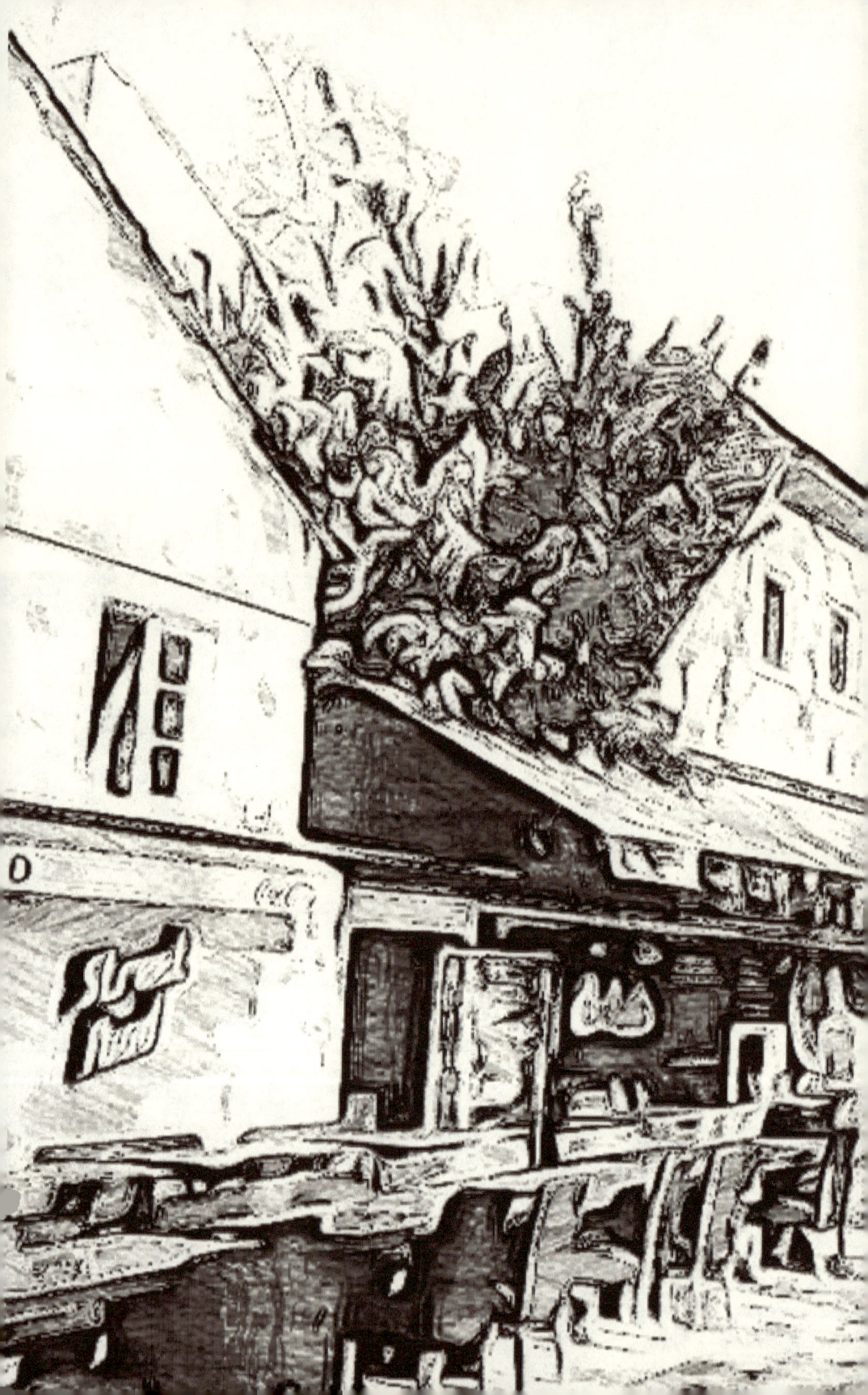

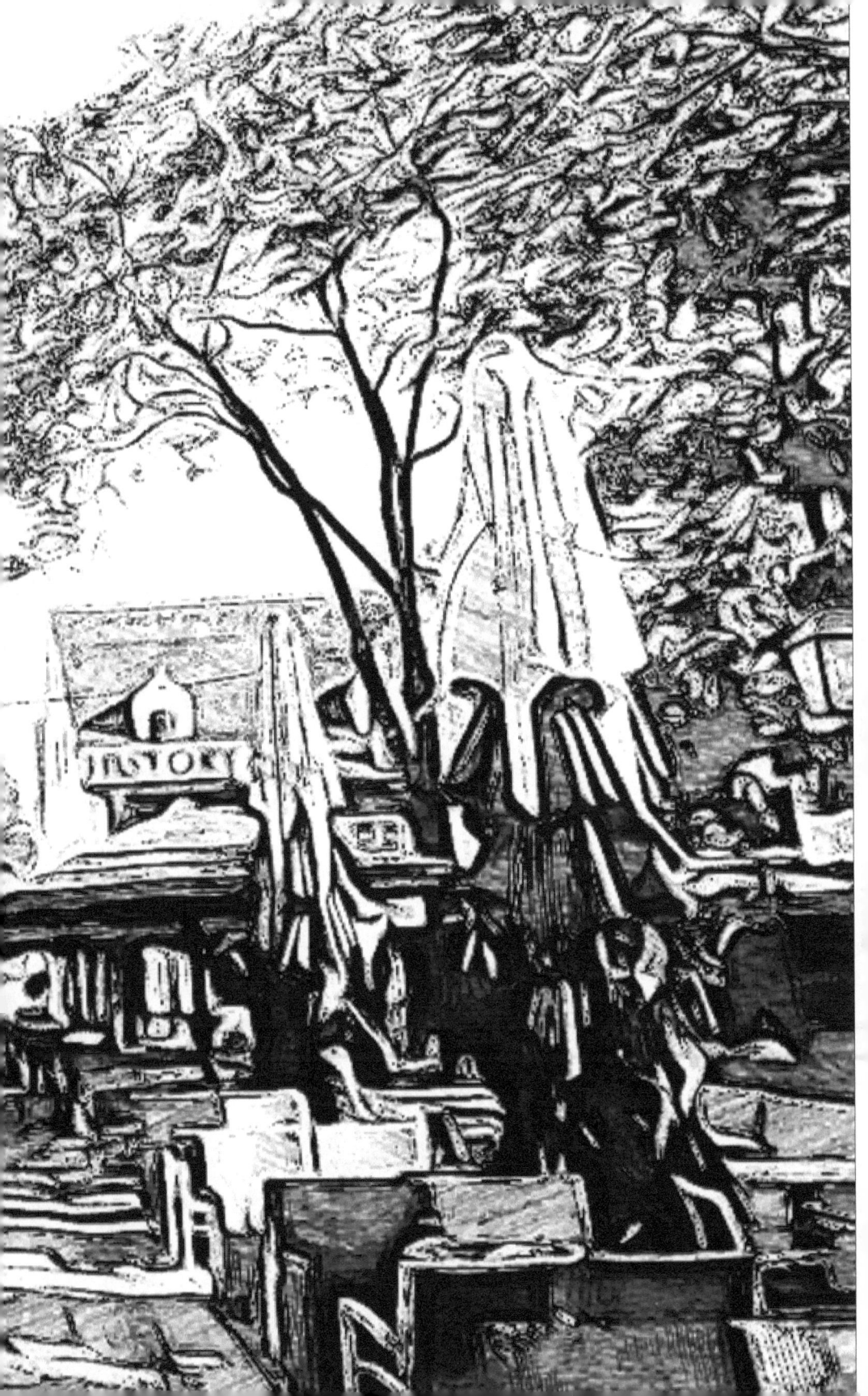

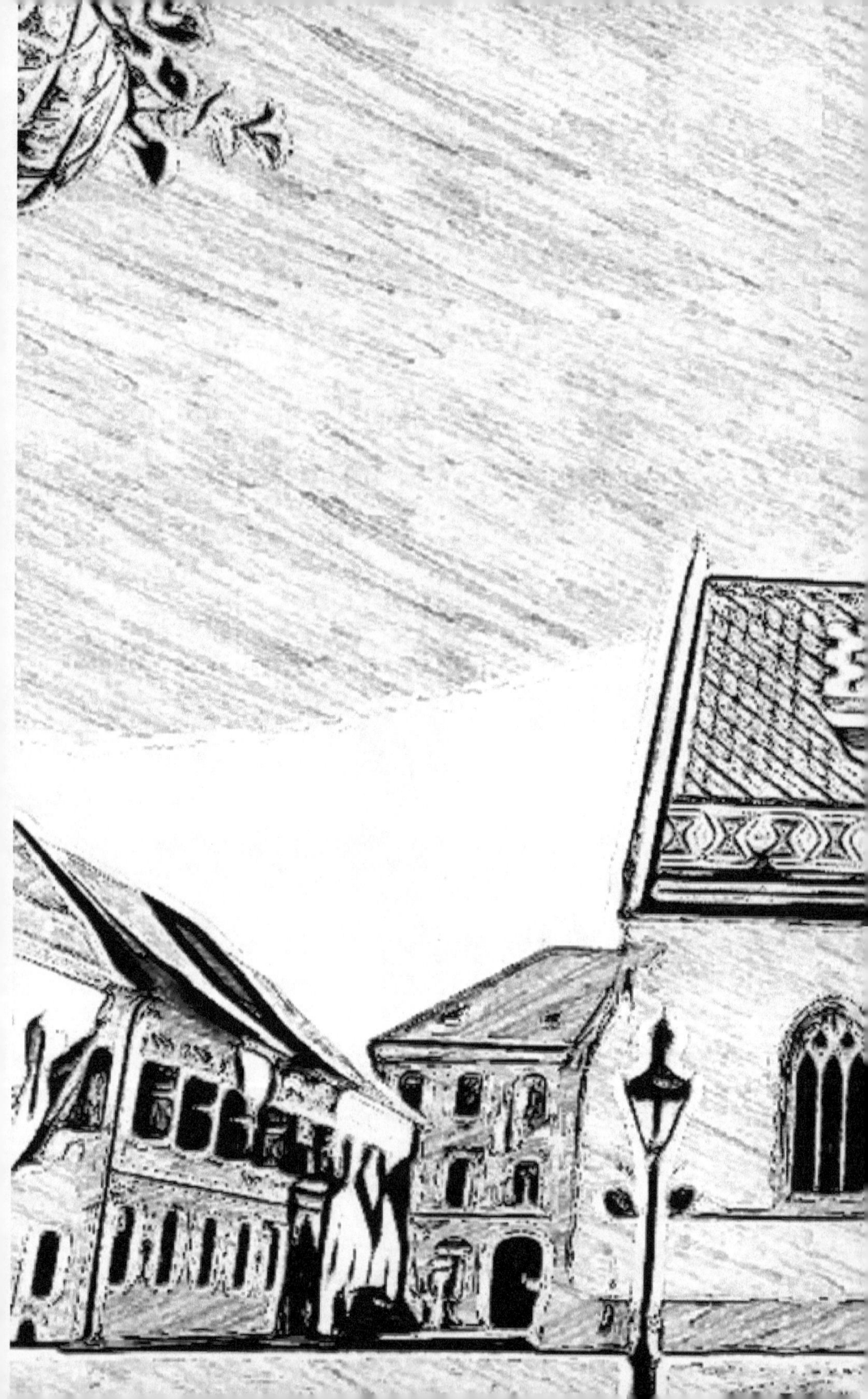

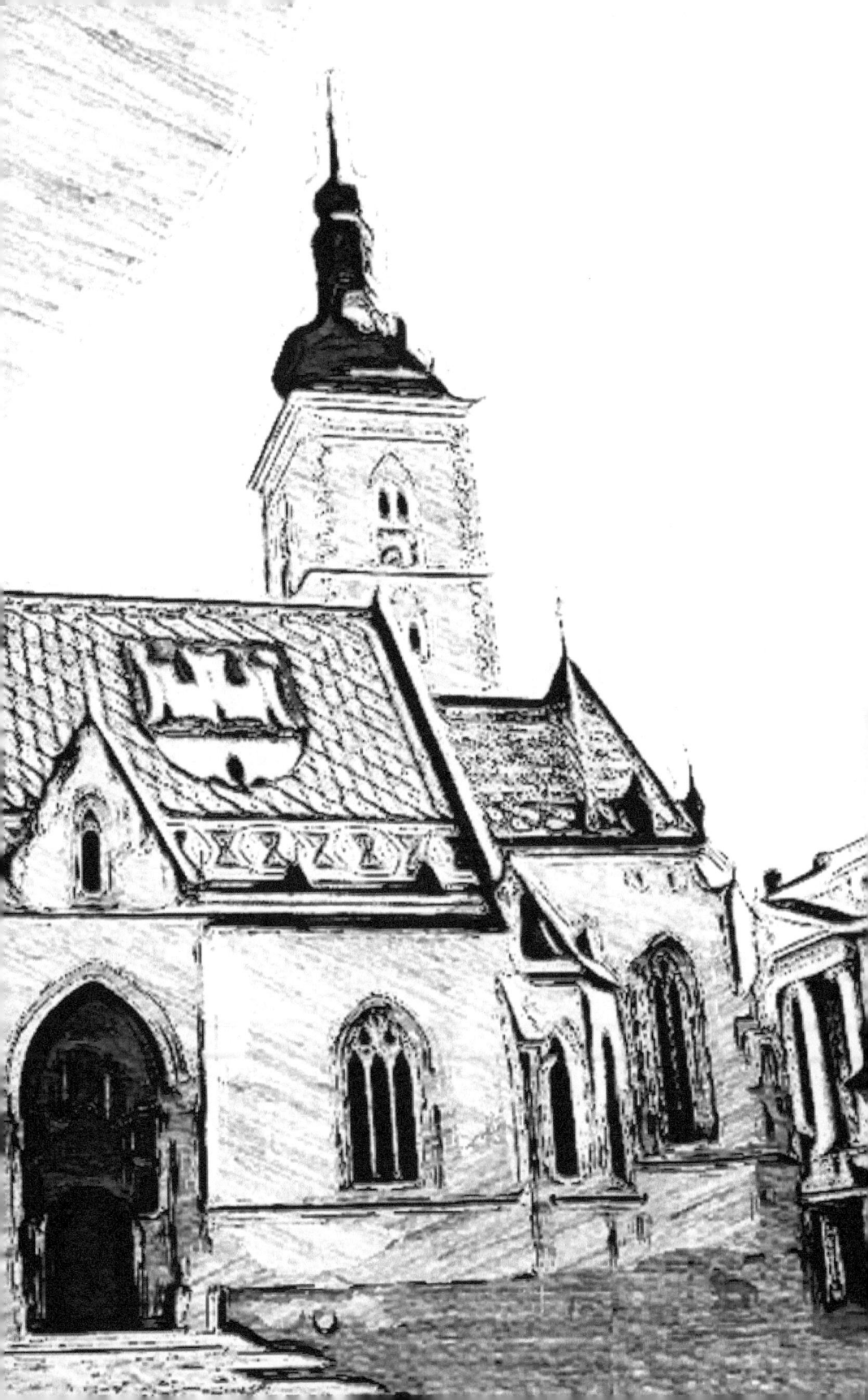

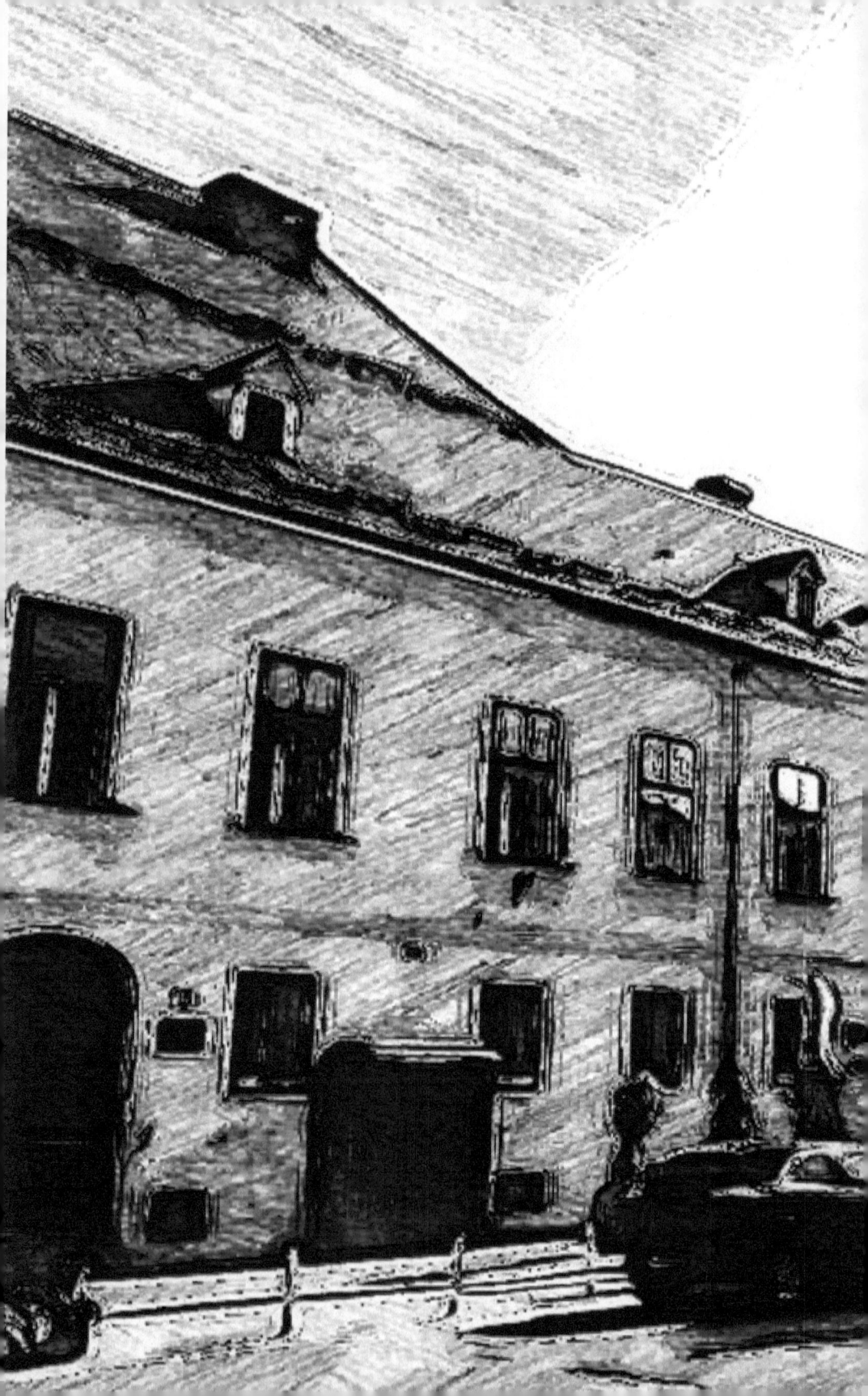

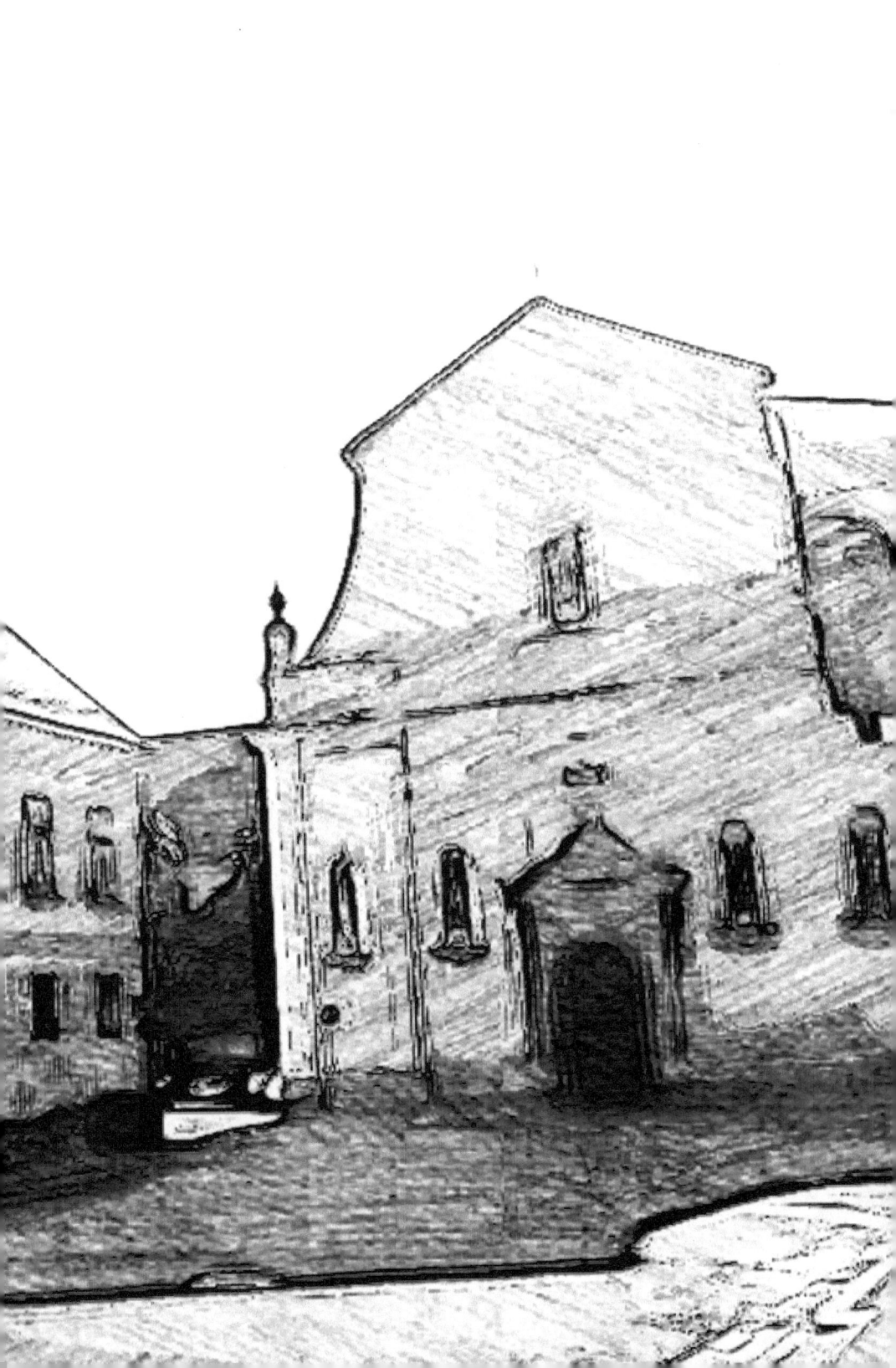

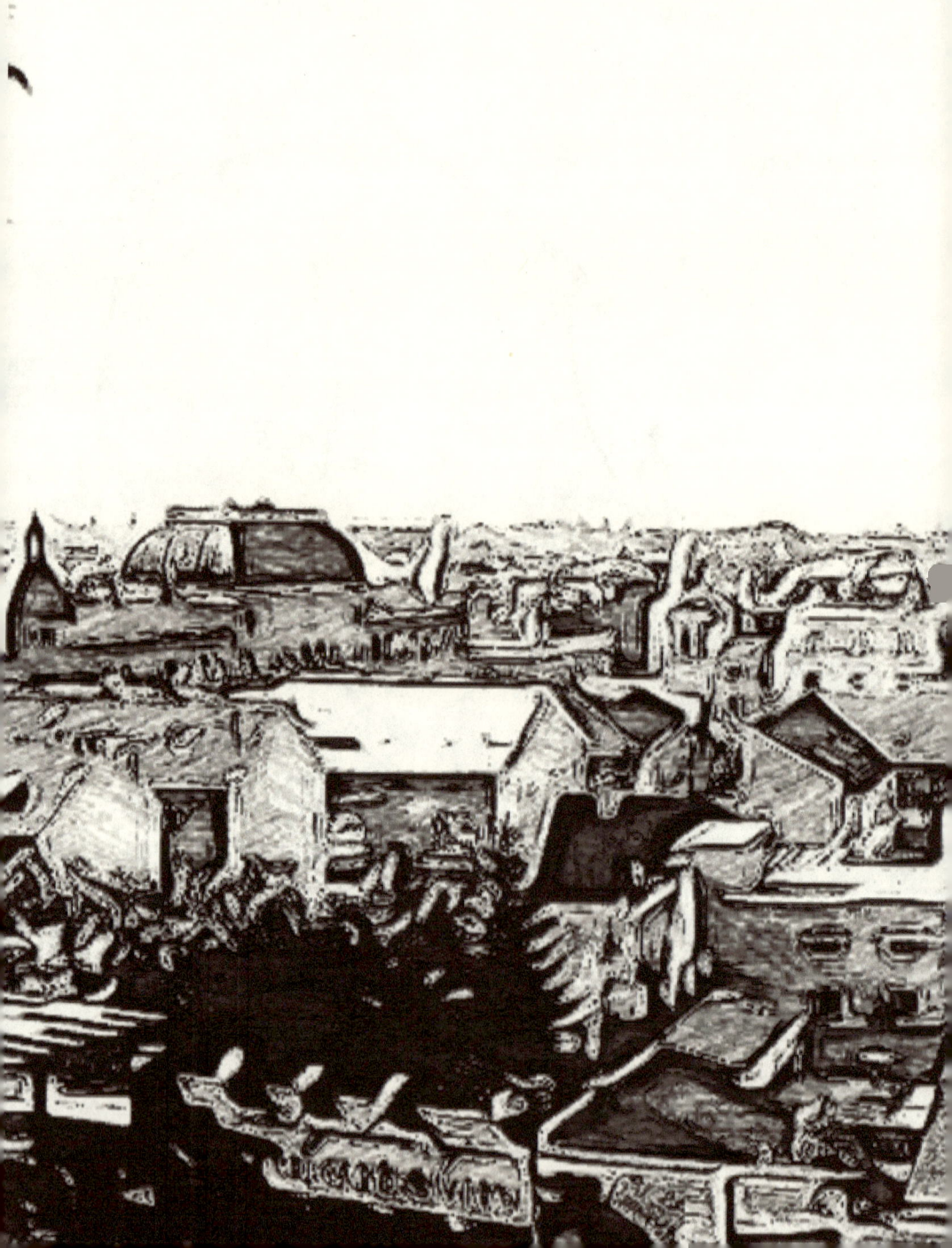

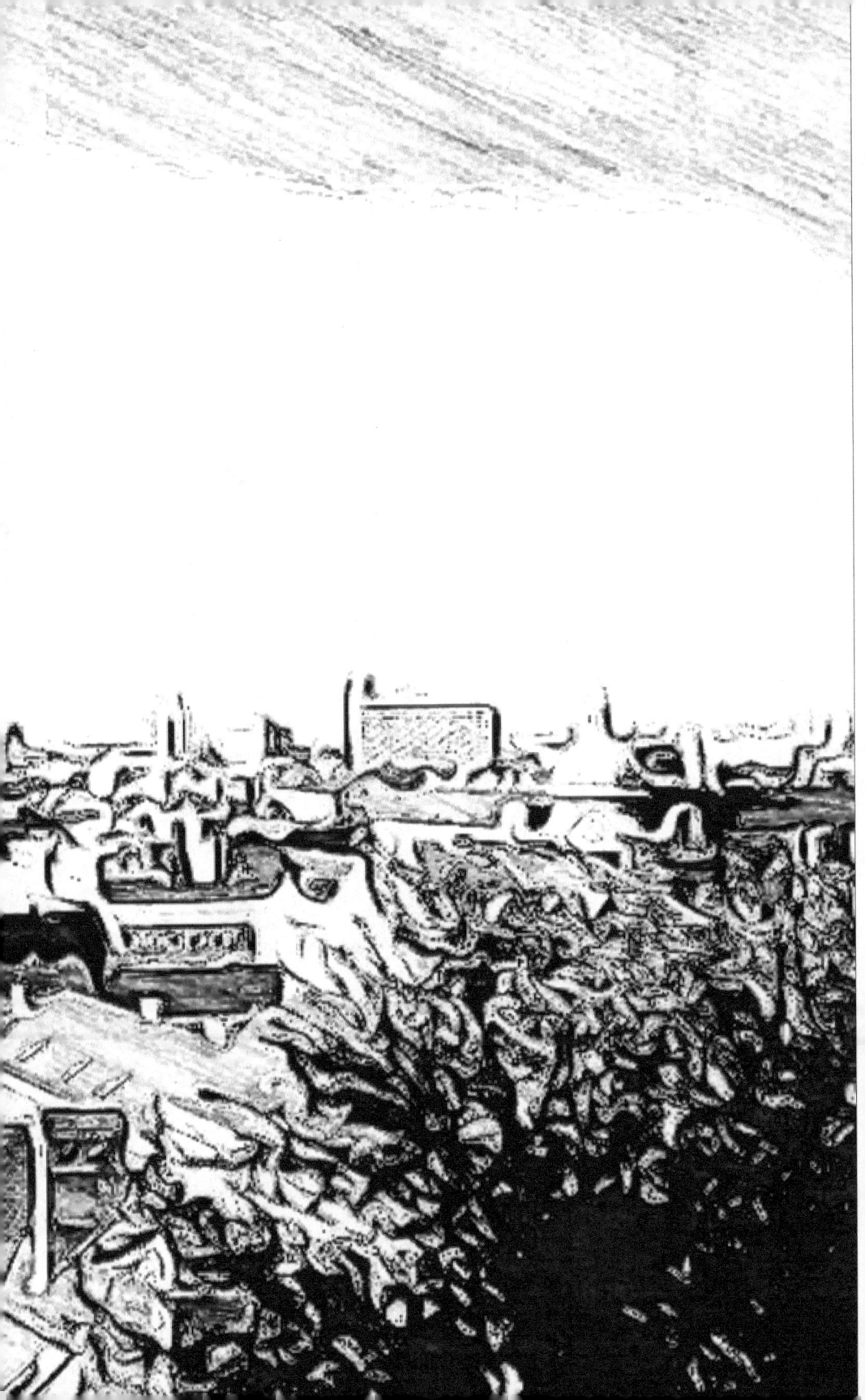

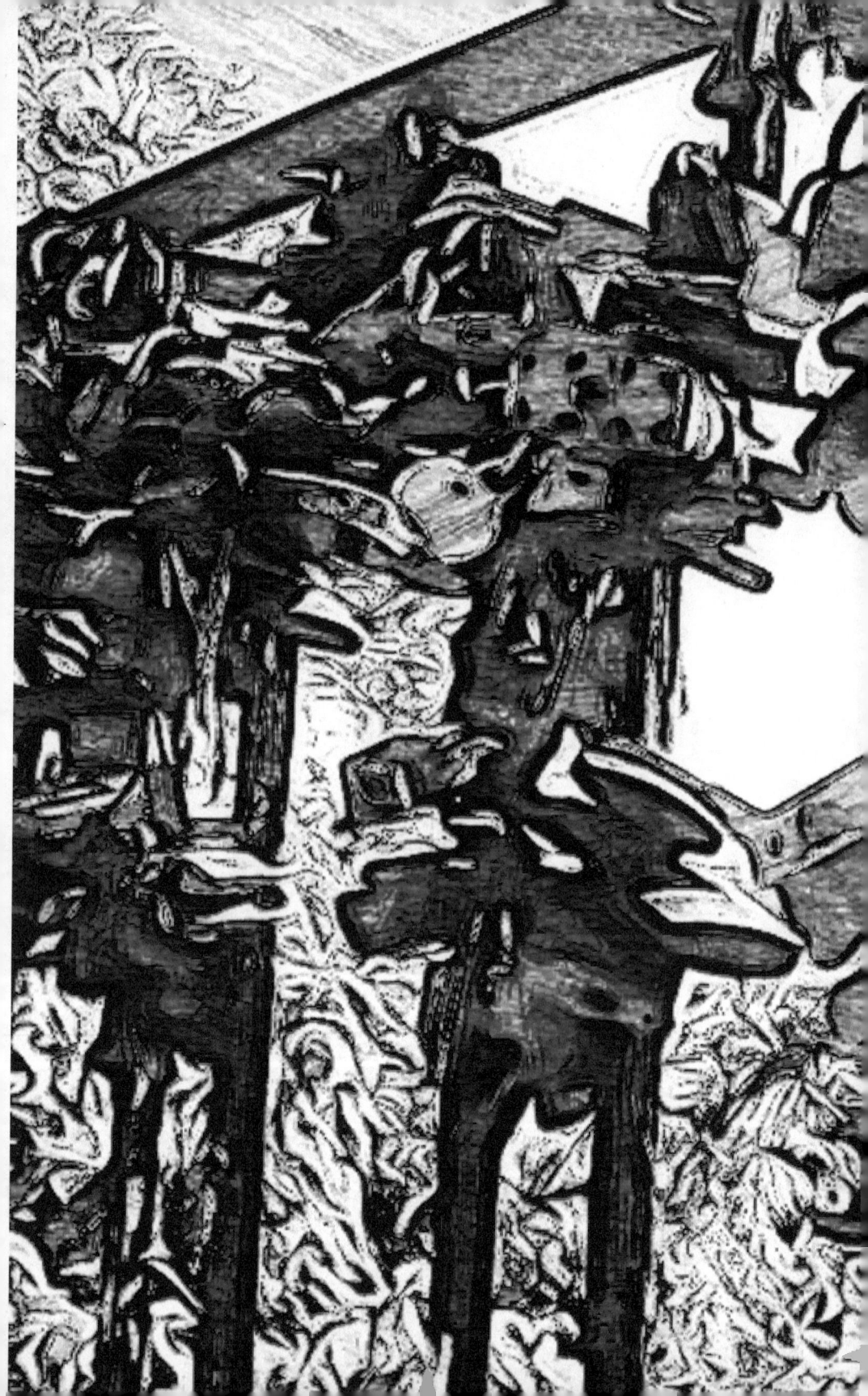

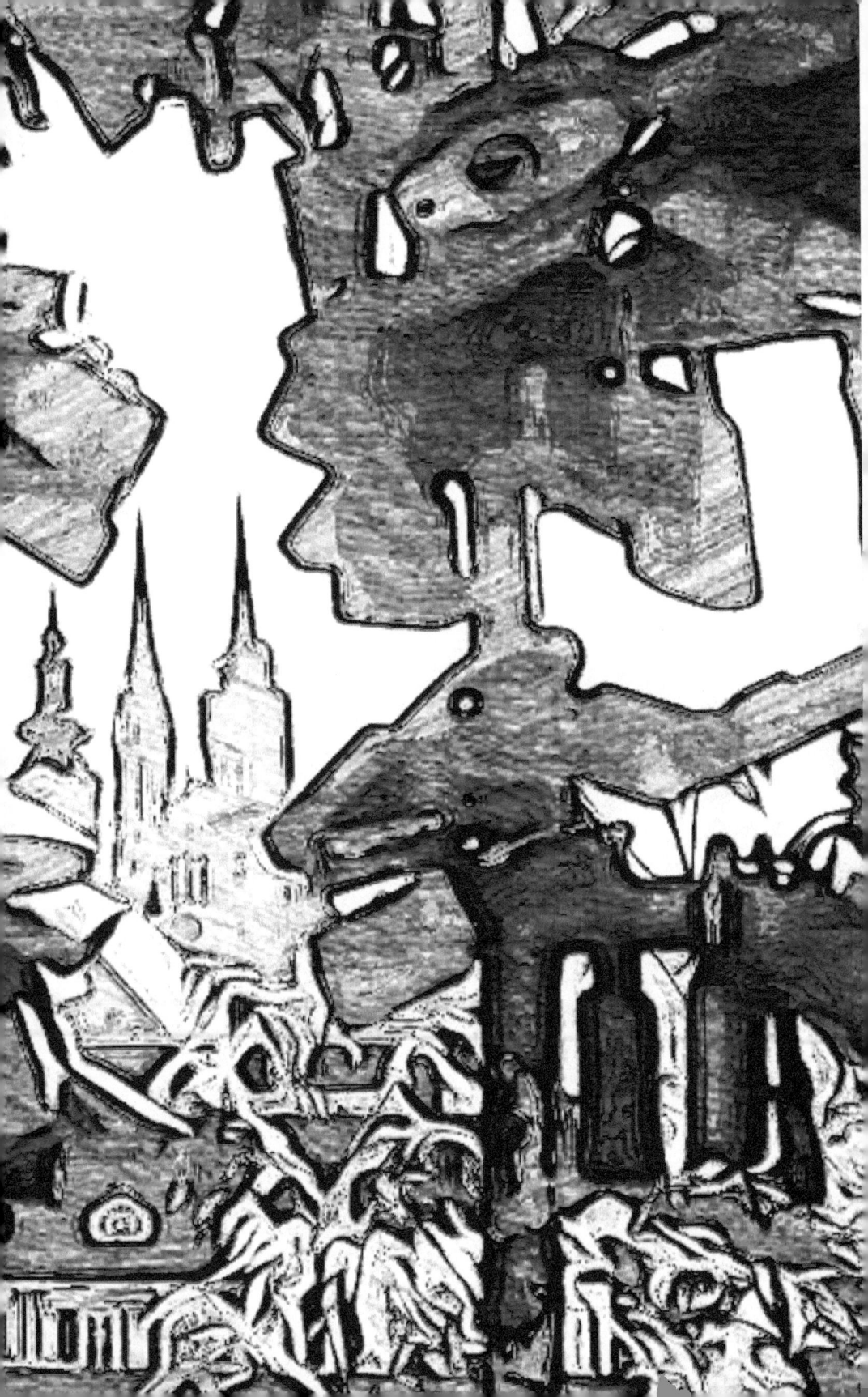

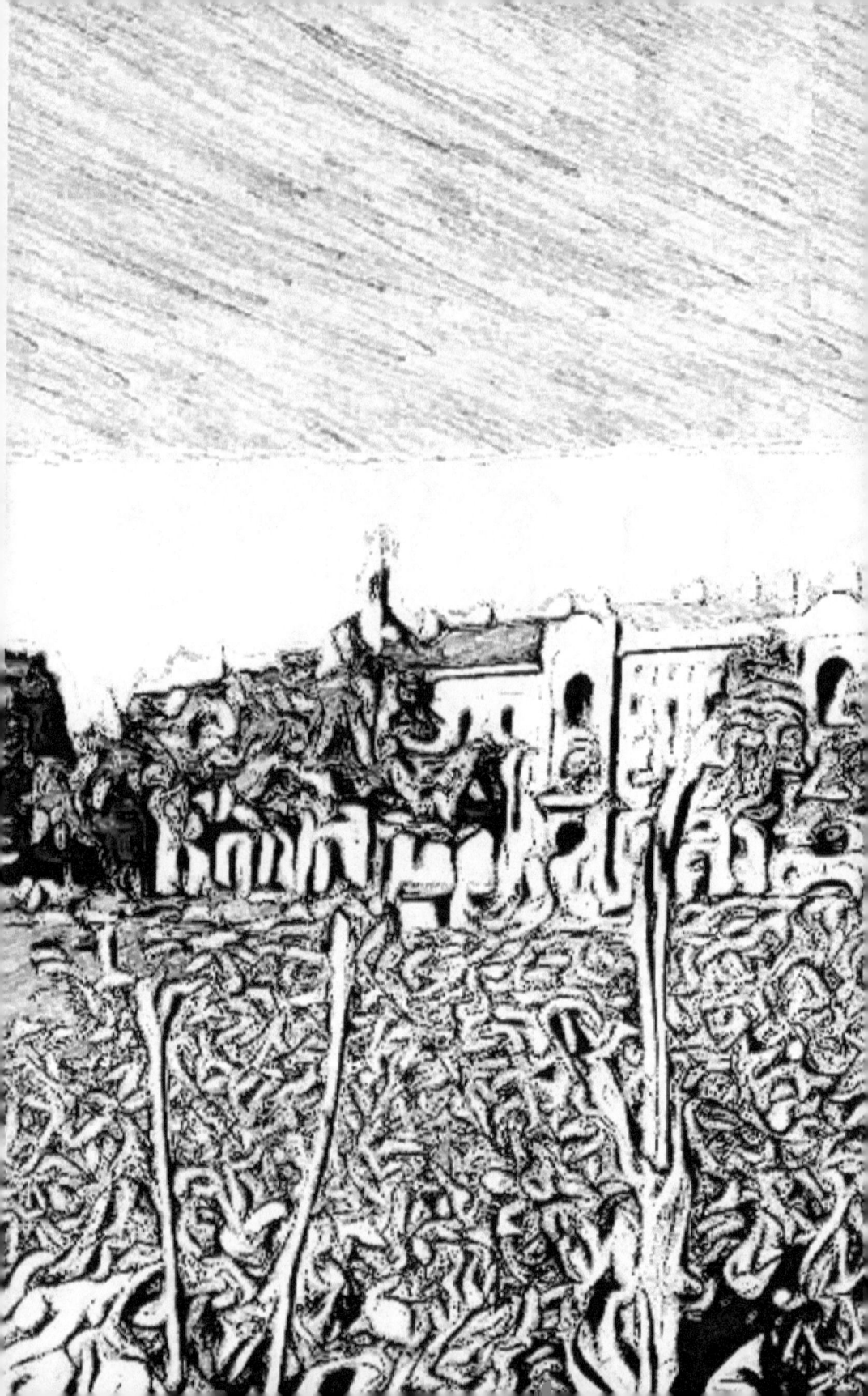

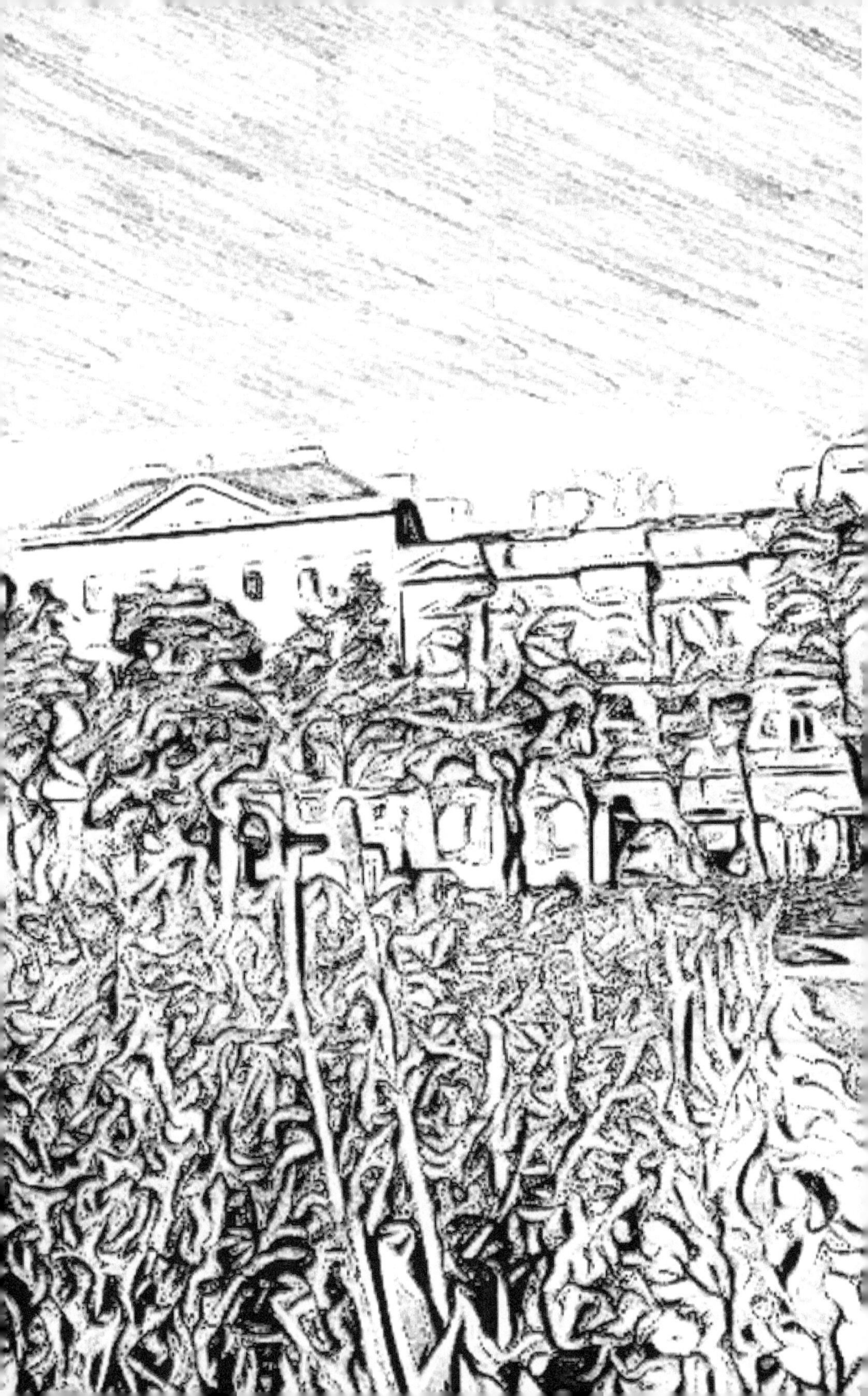

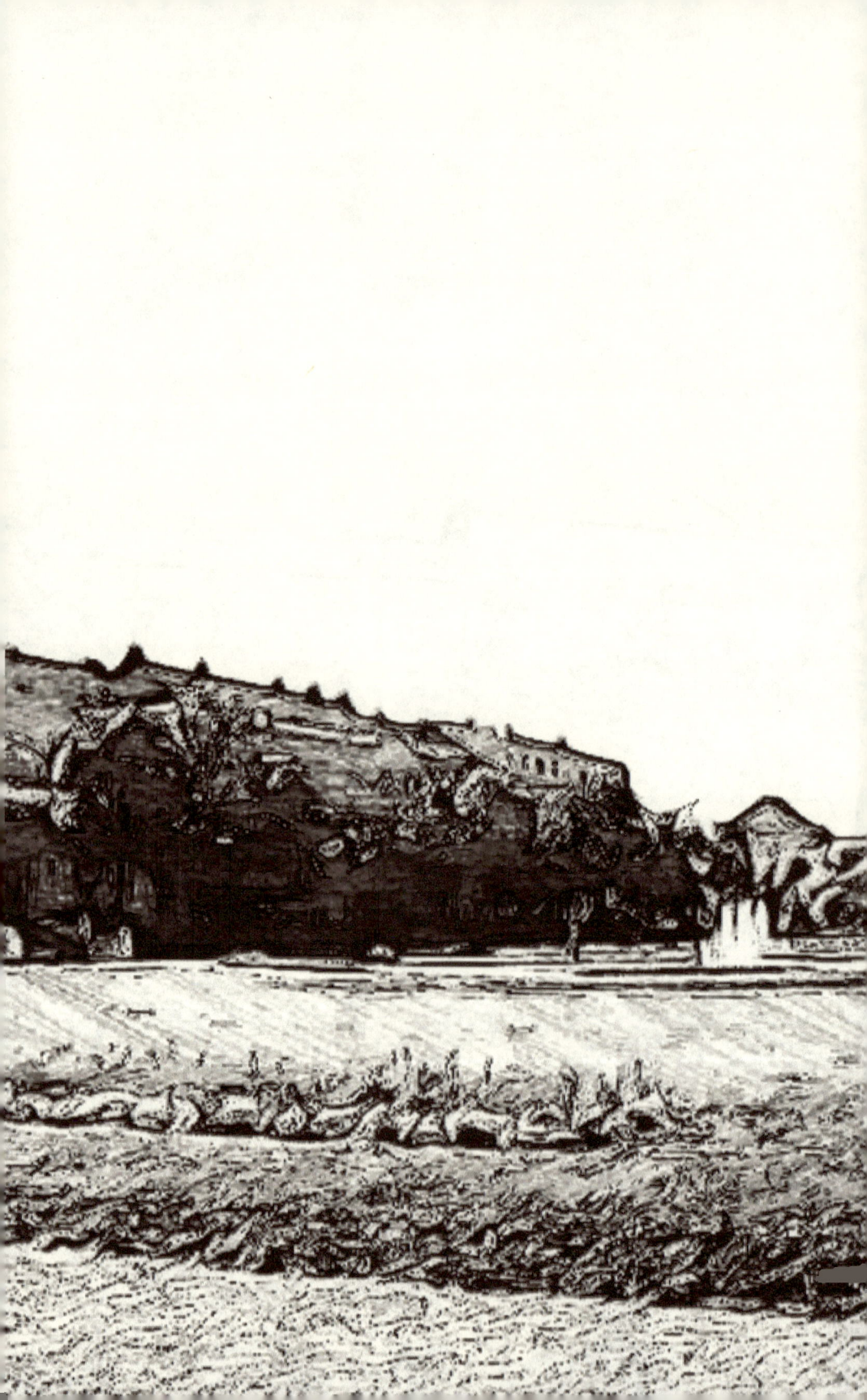

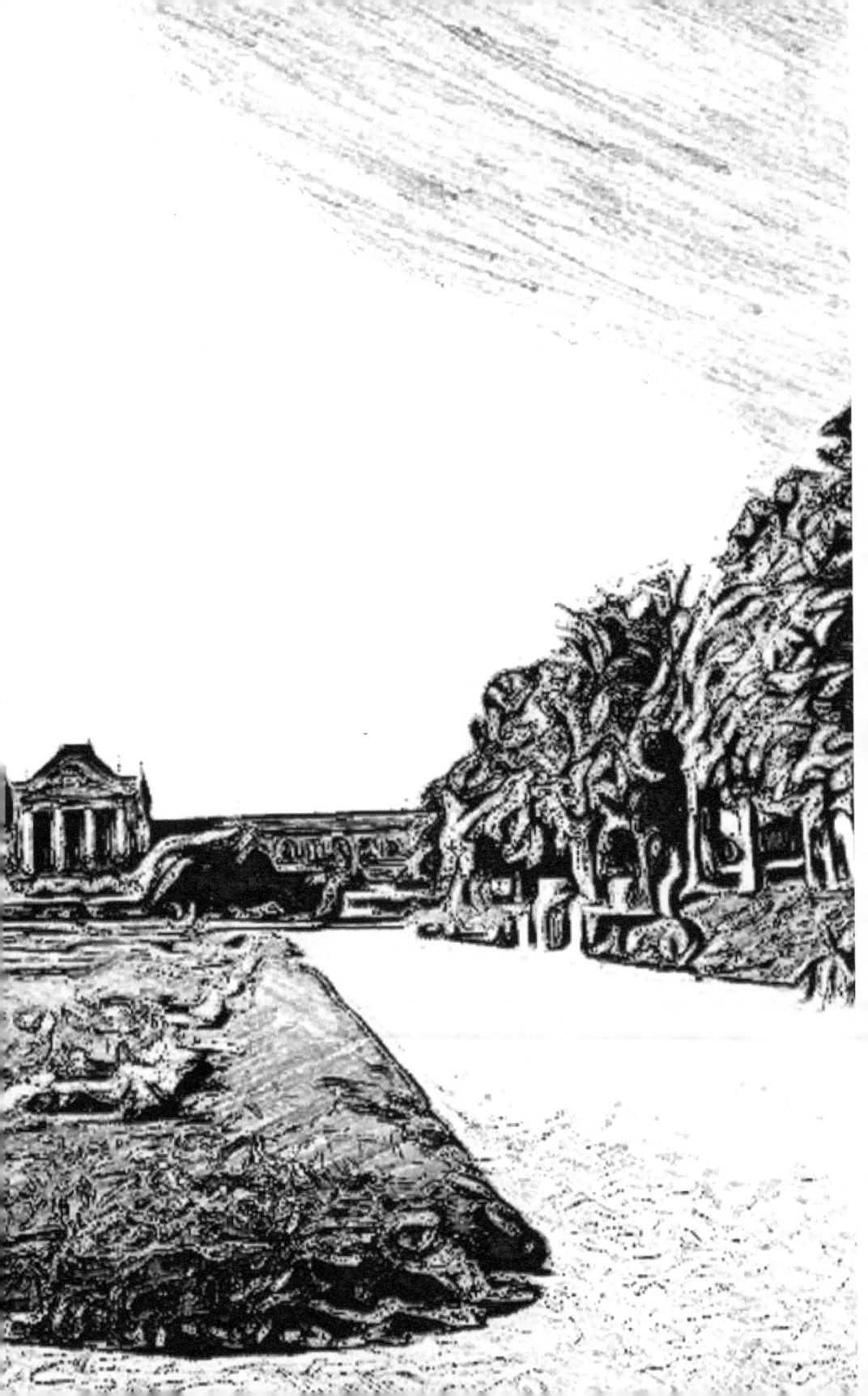

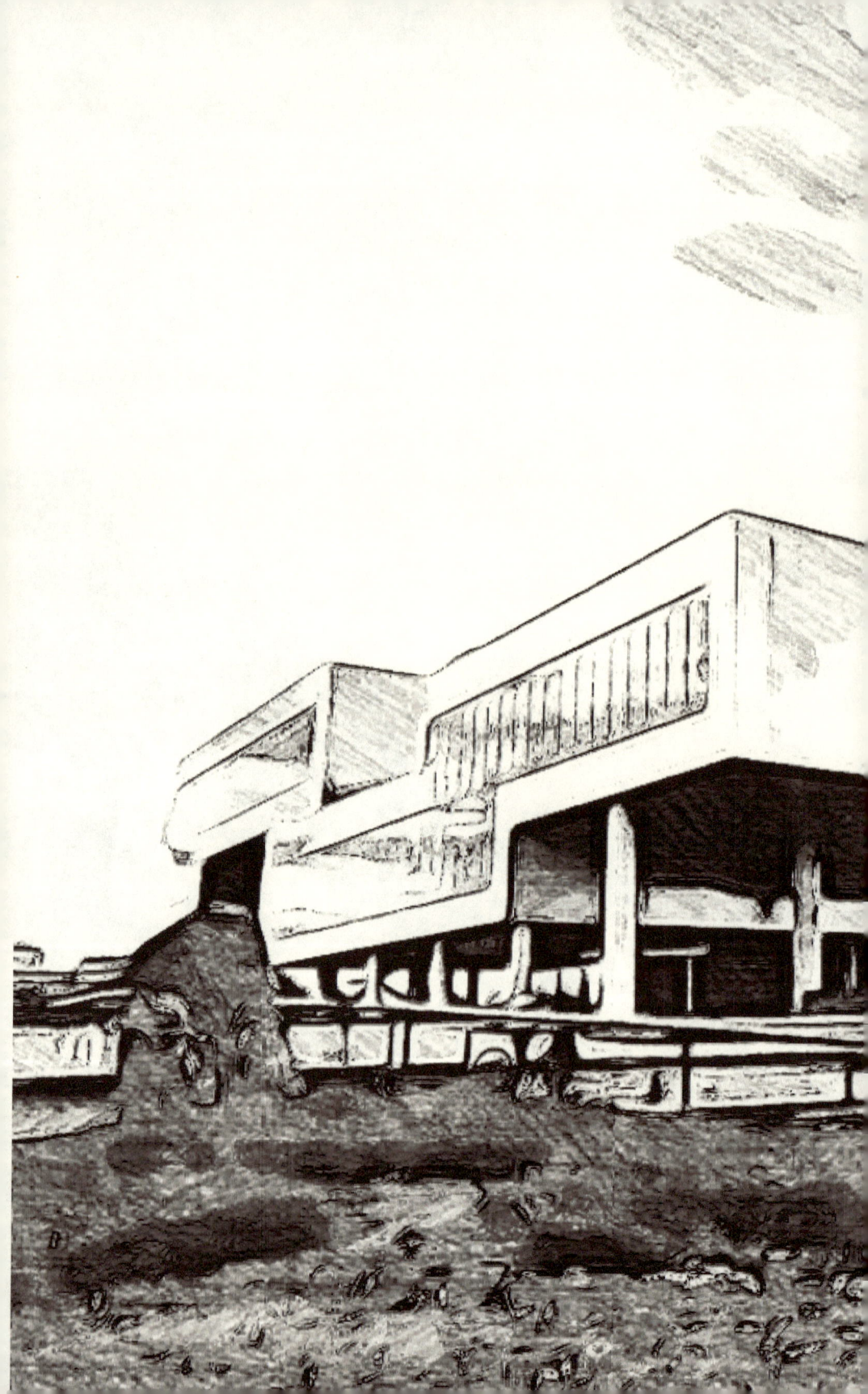

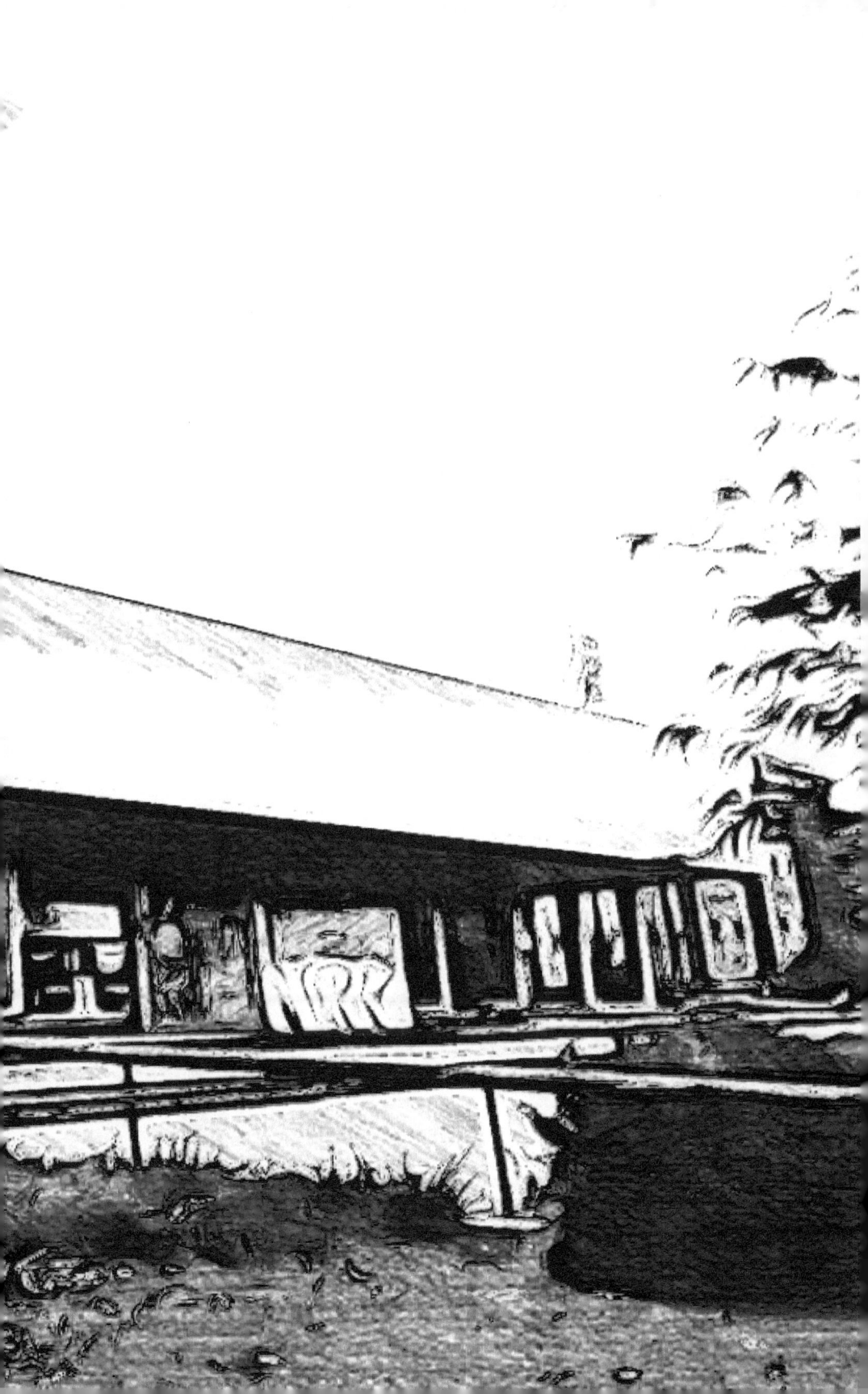

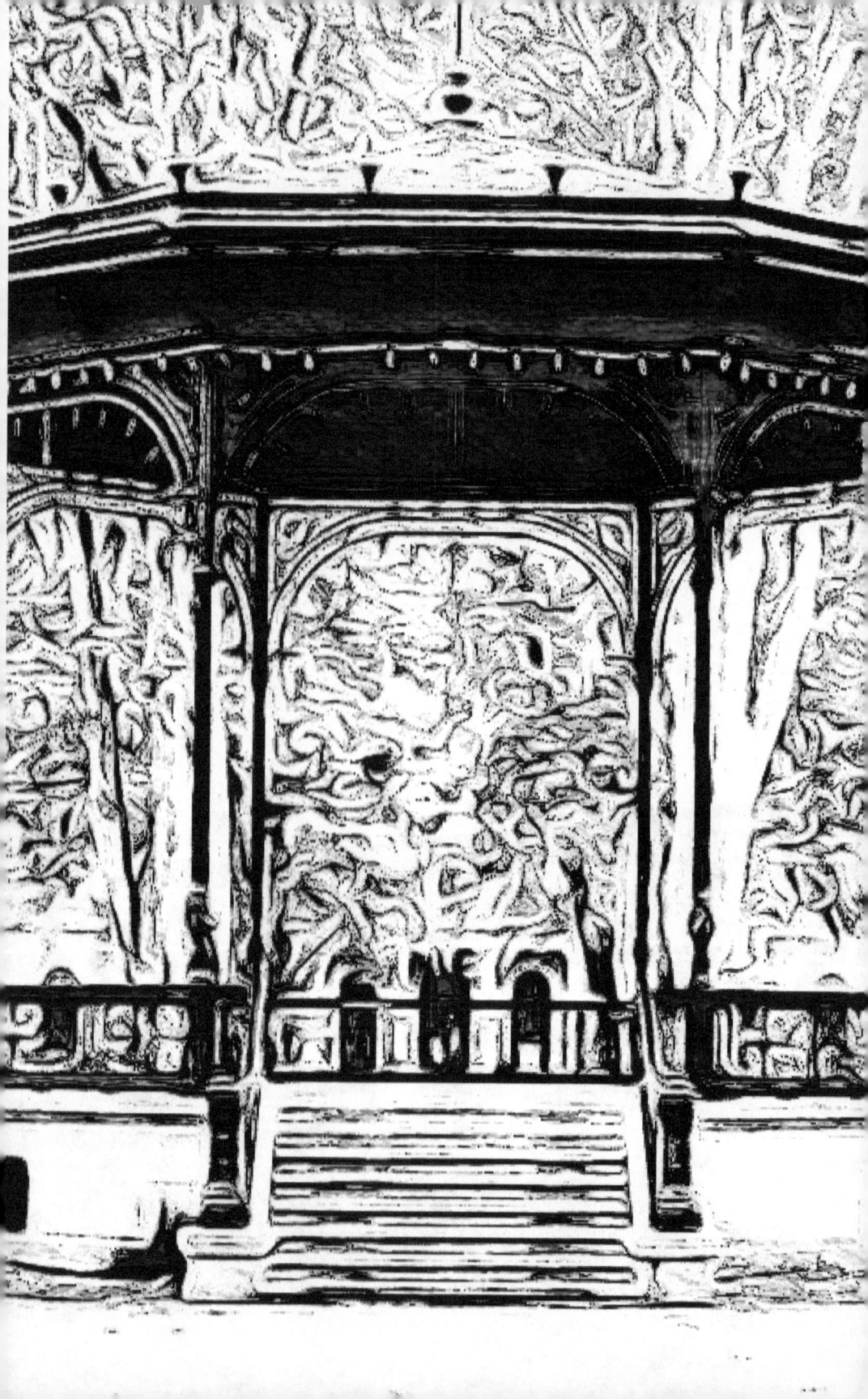

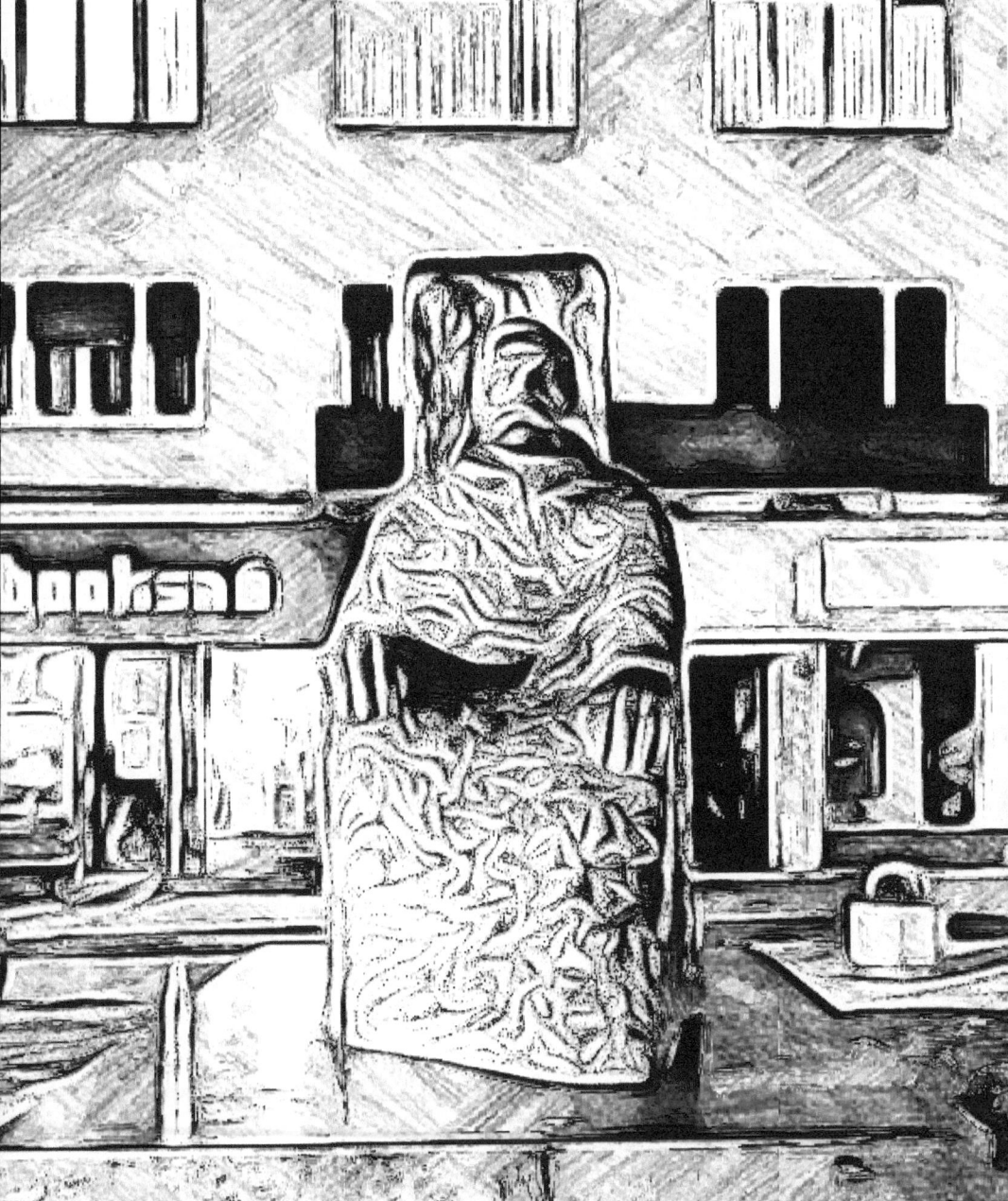

FRA GRGO MARTIC

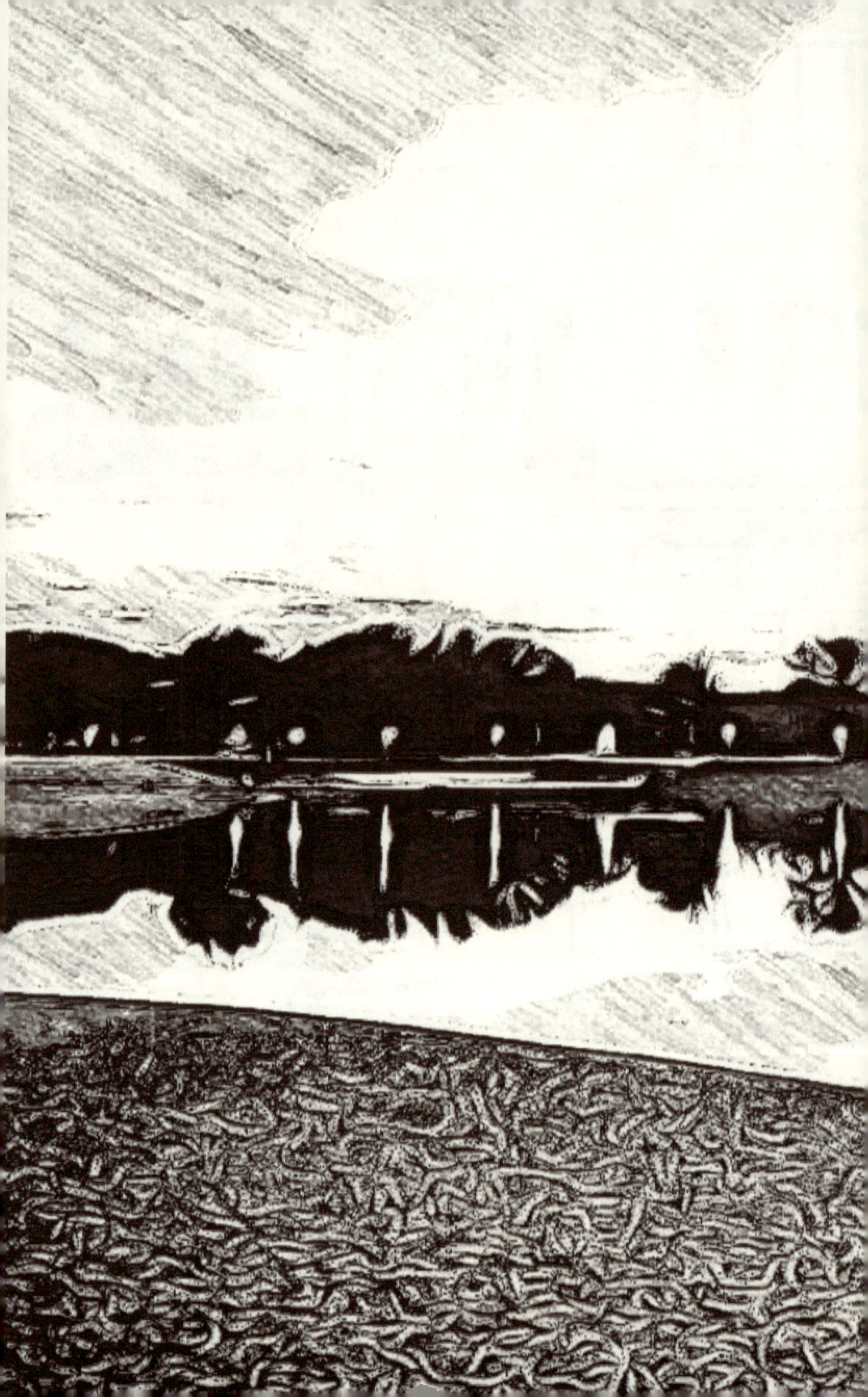

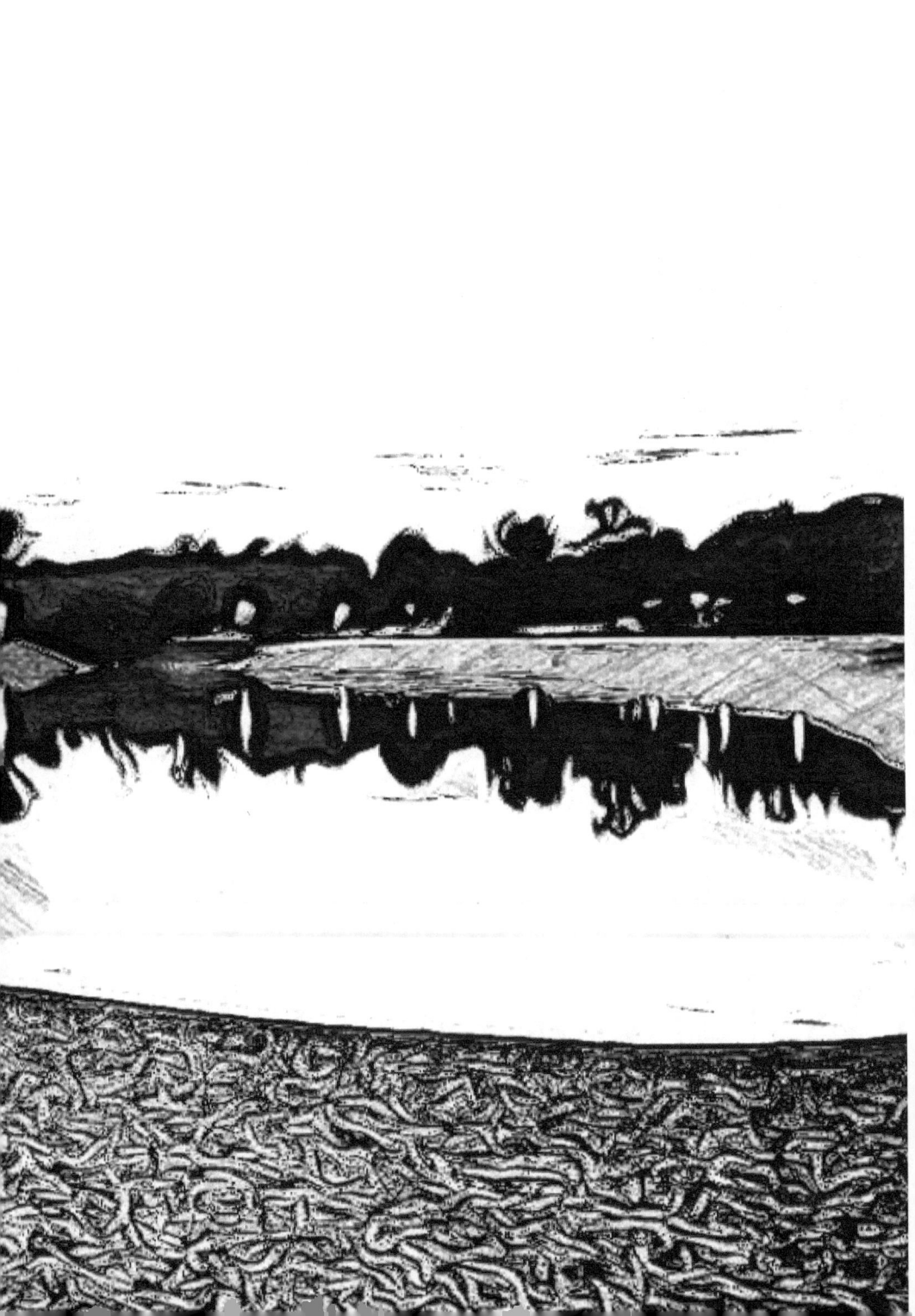

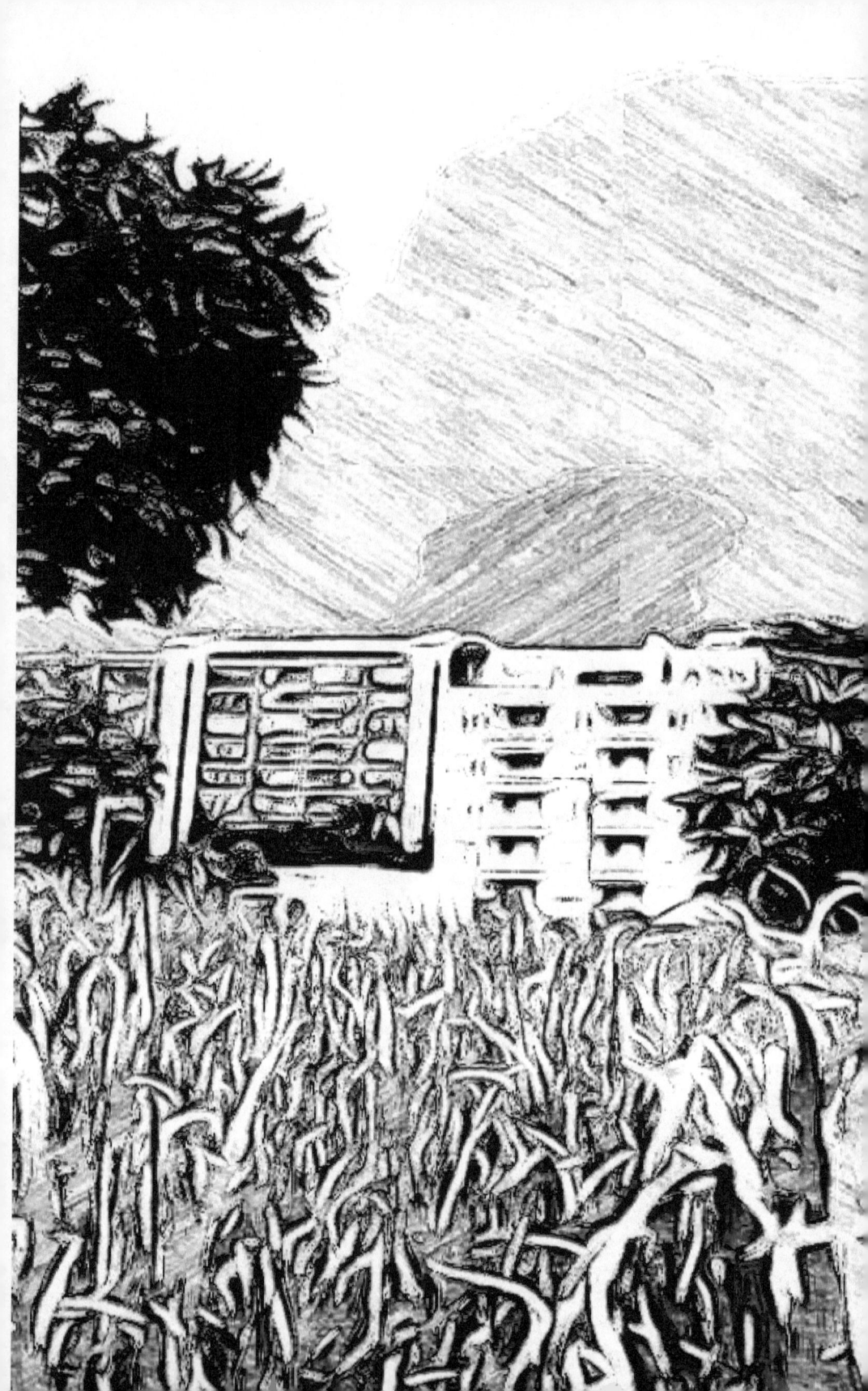

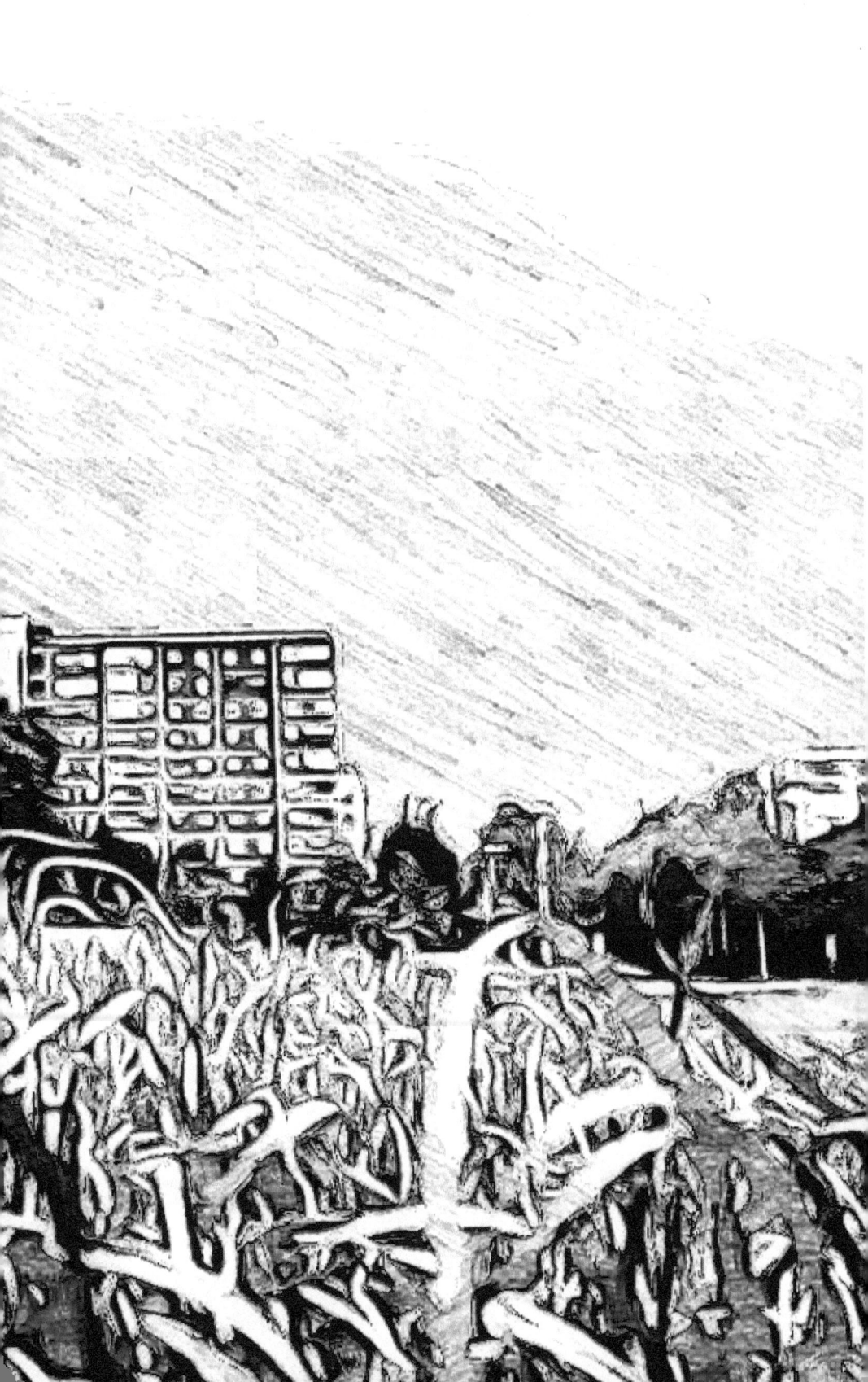

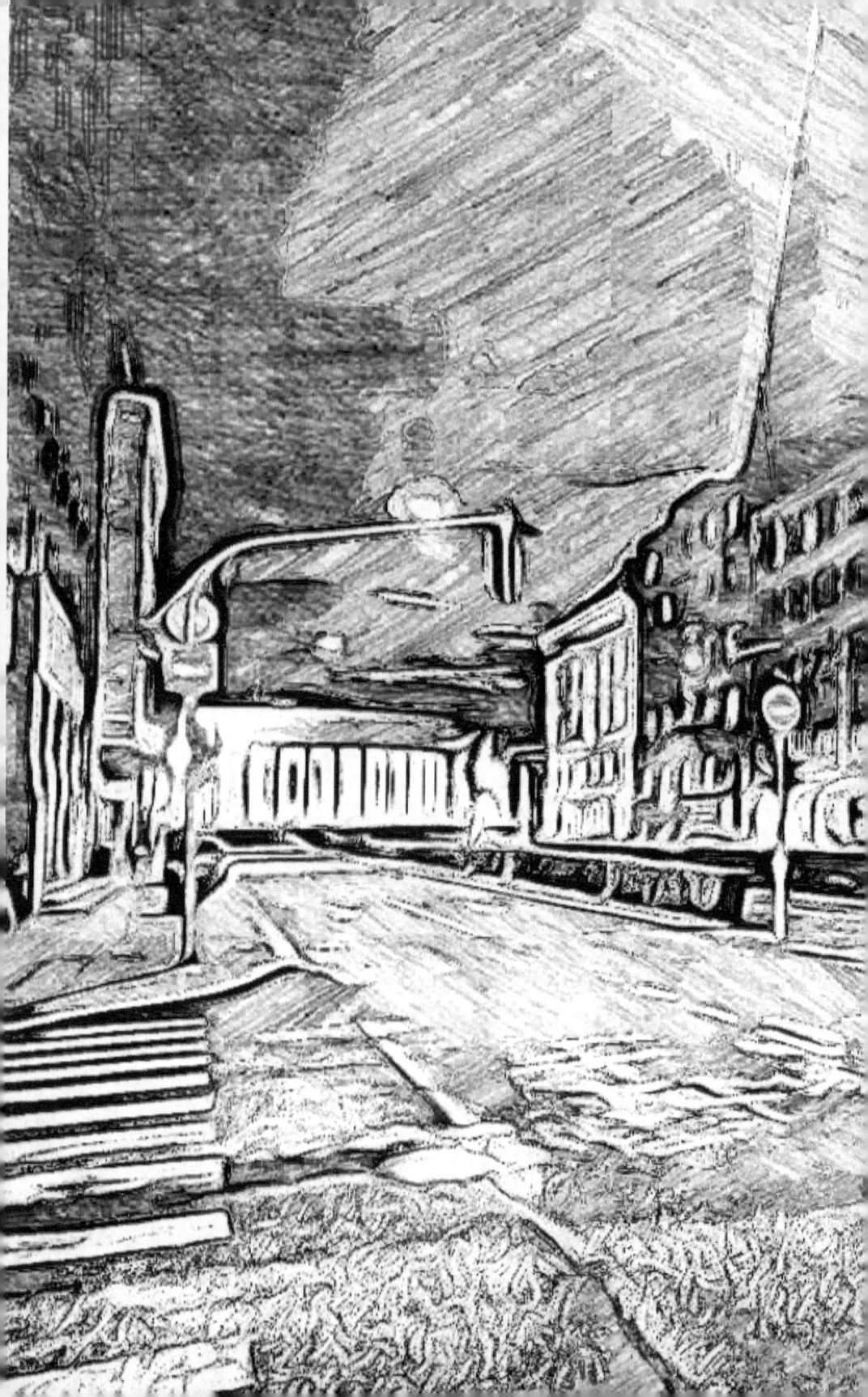

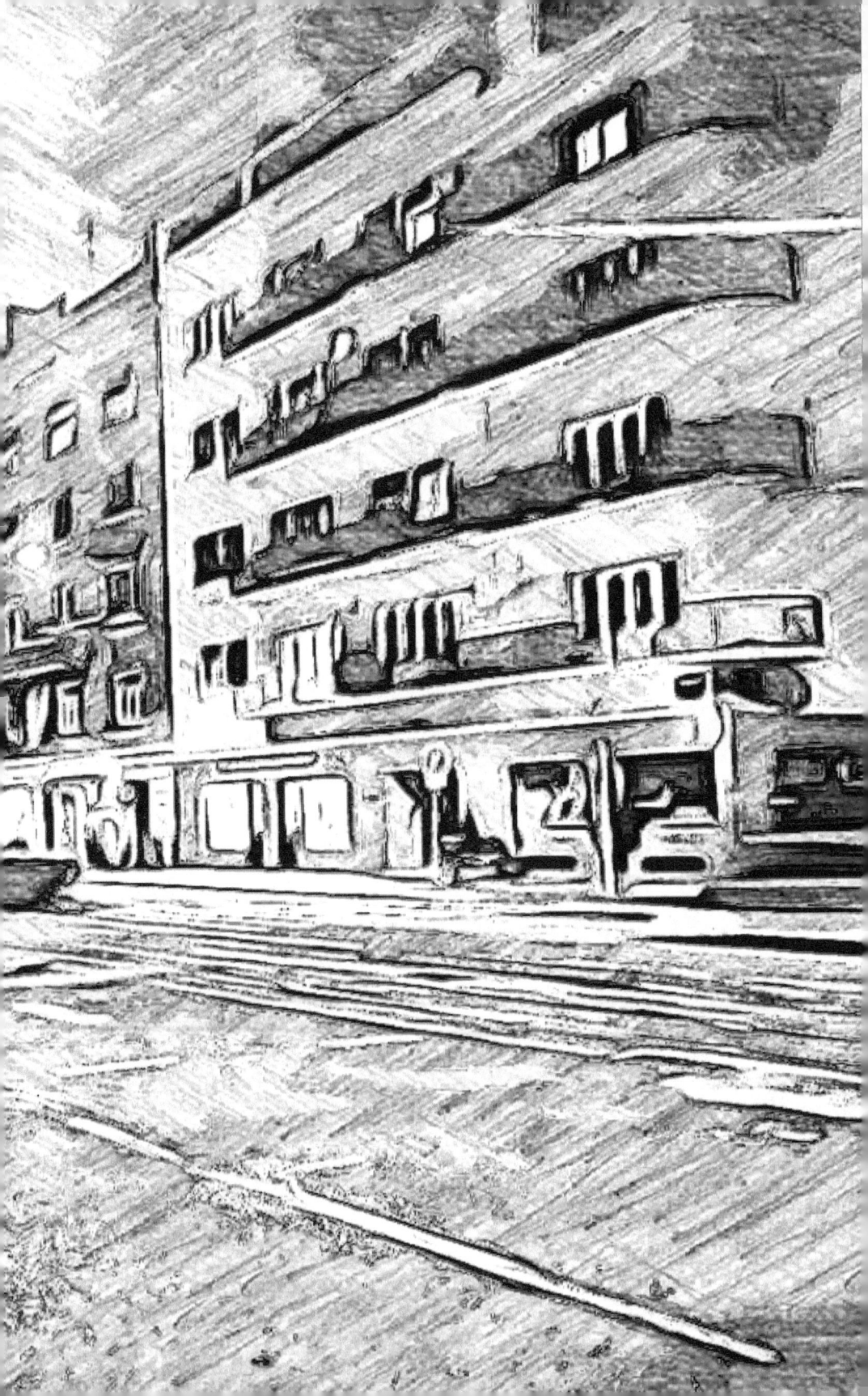

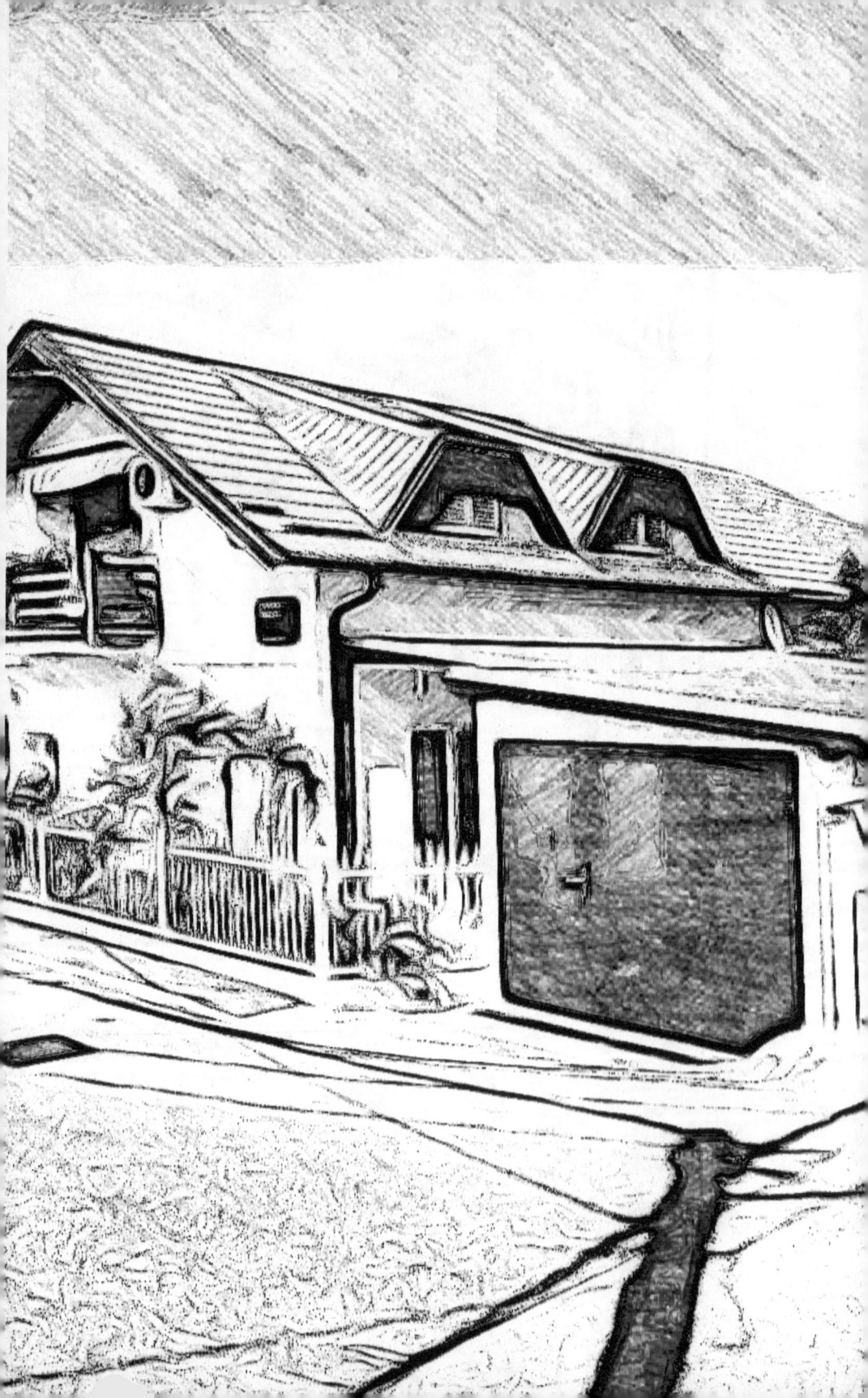

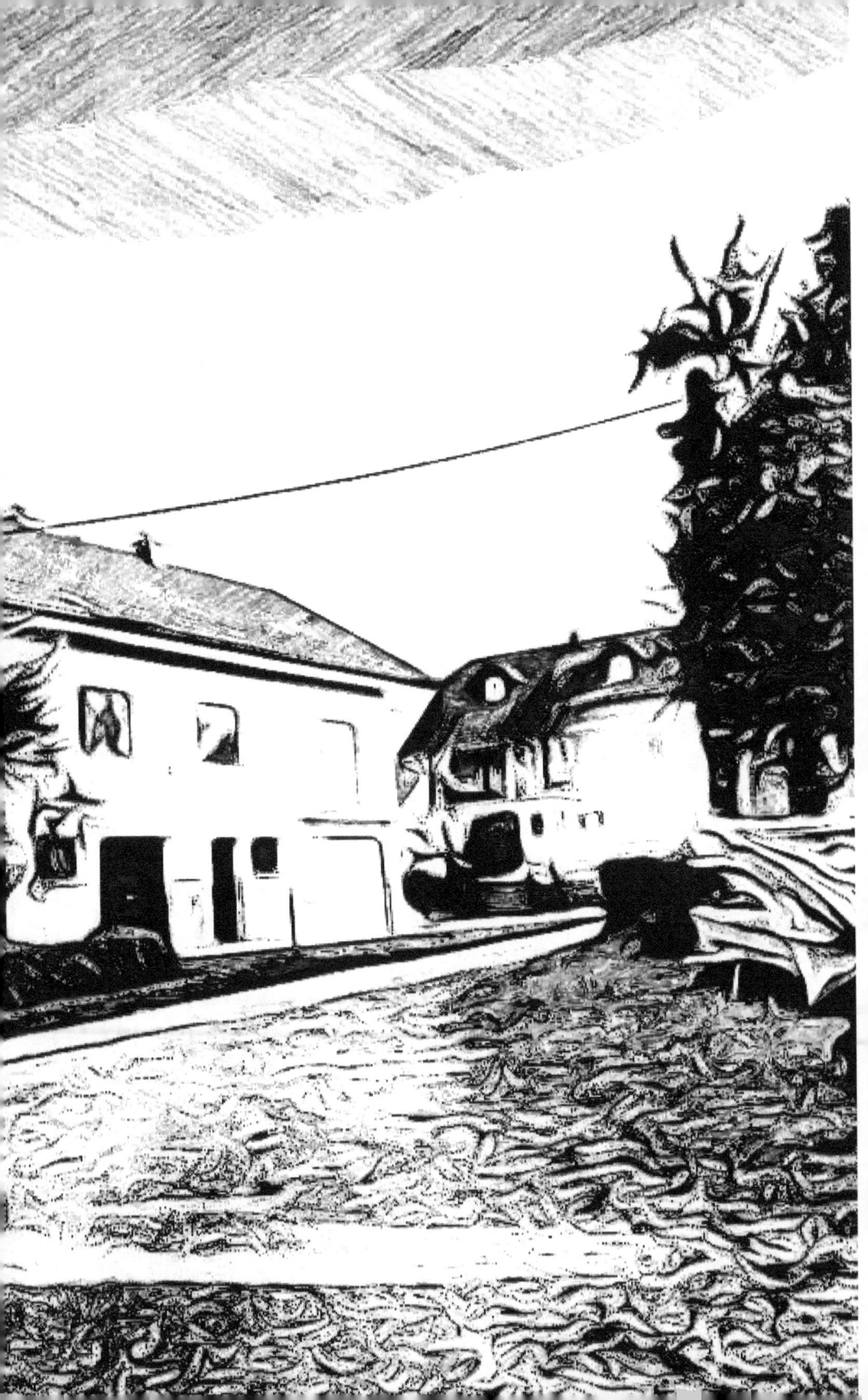

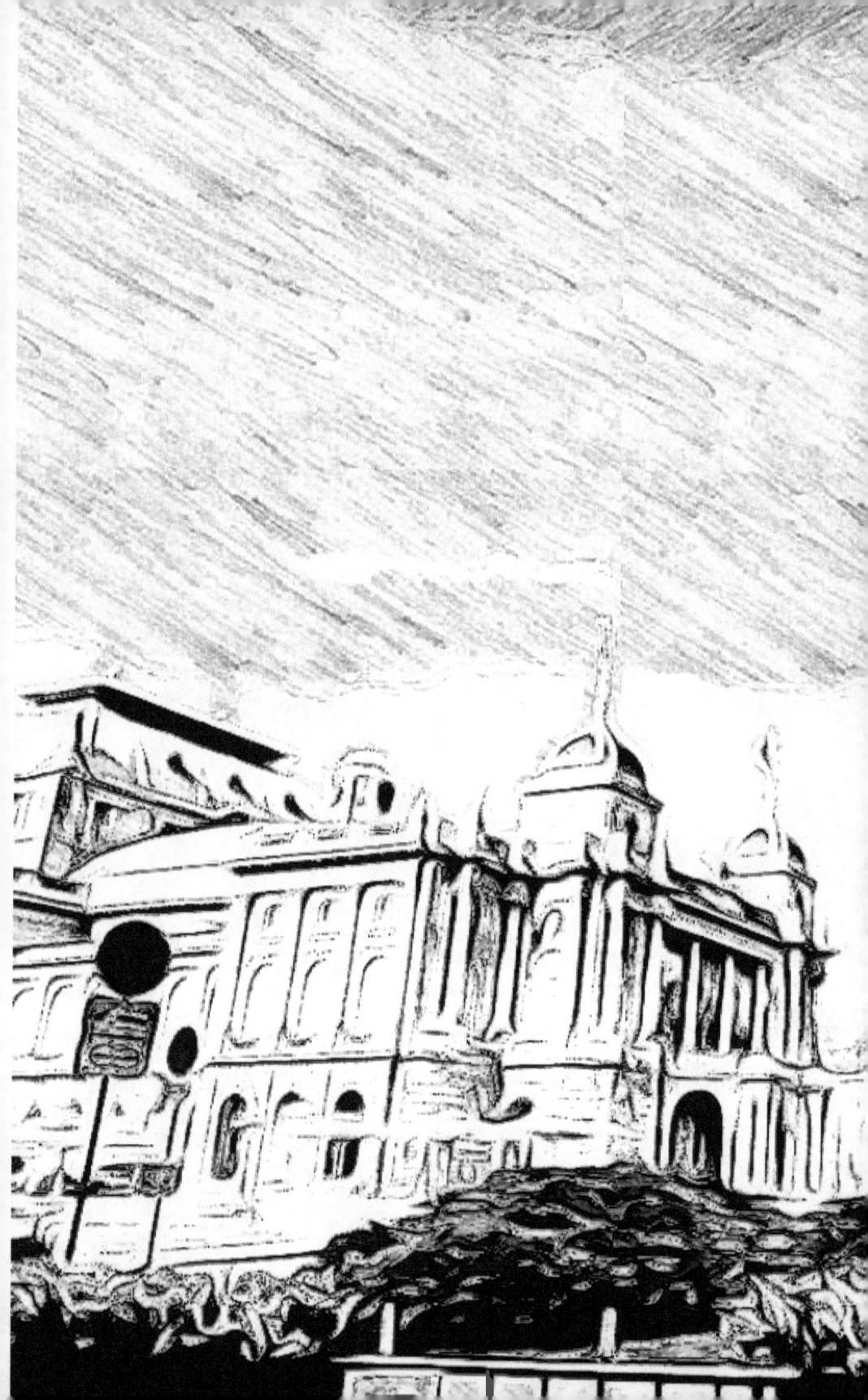

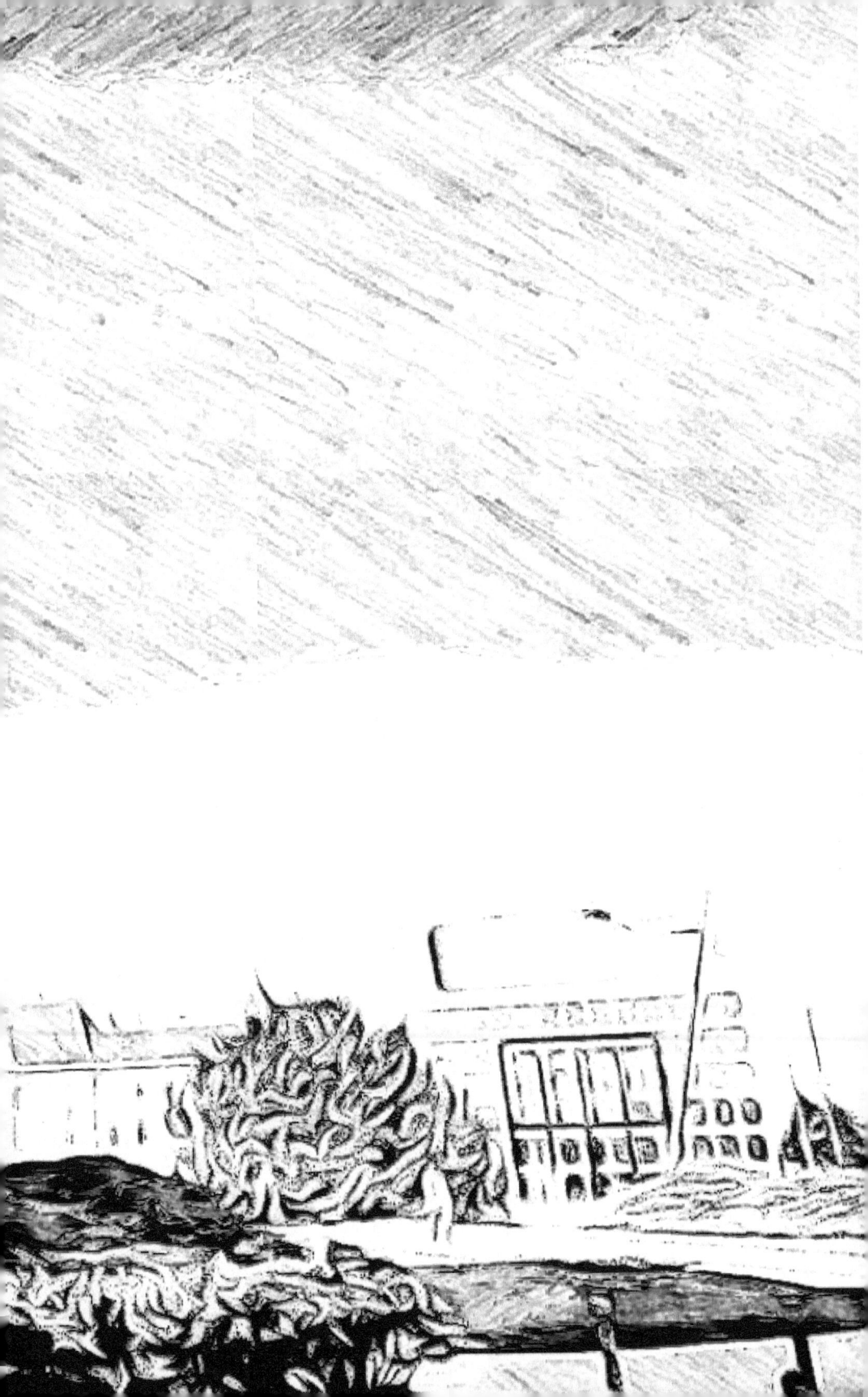

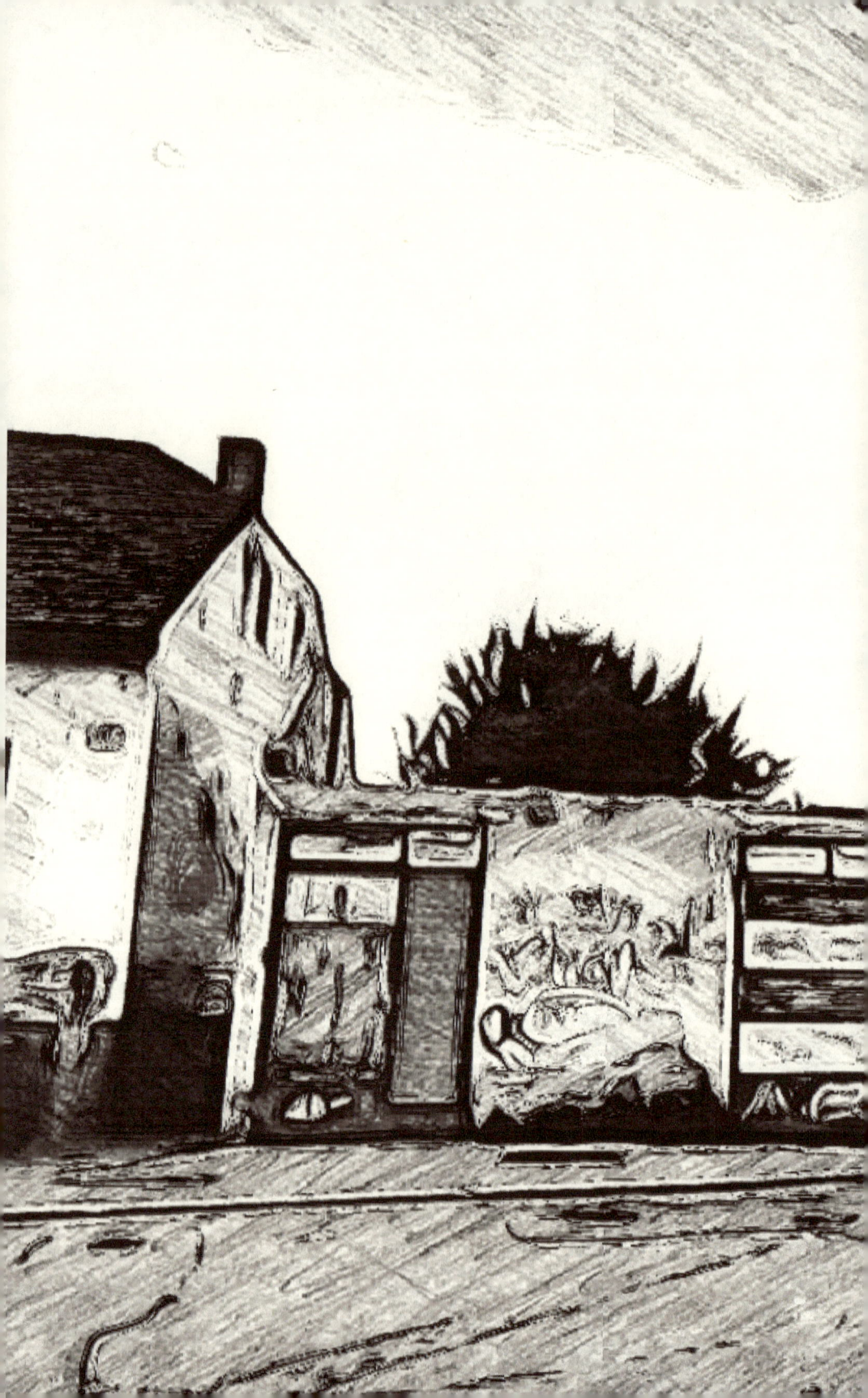

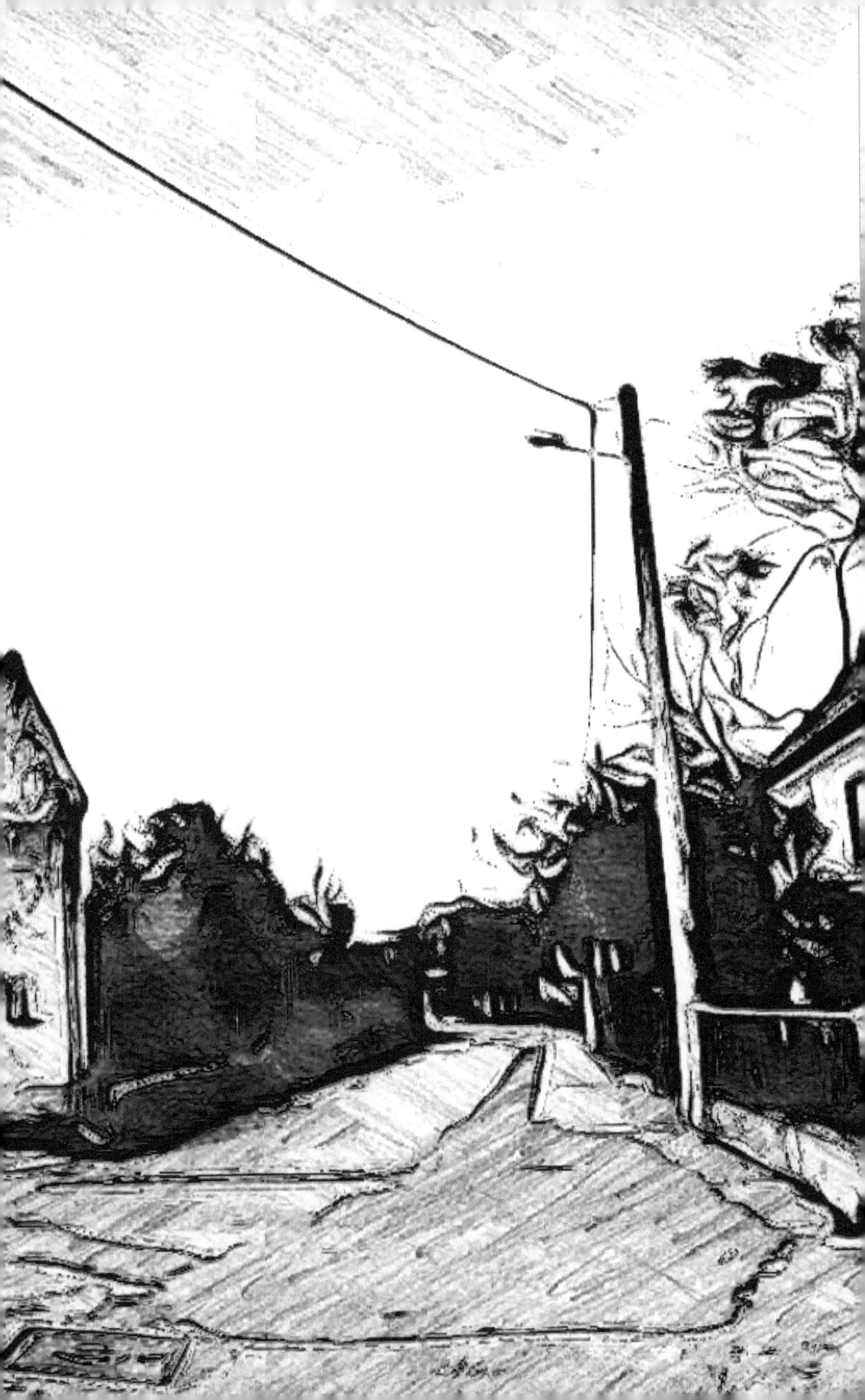

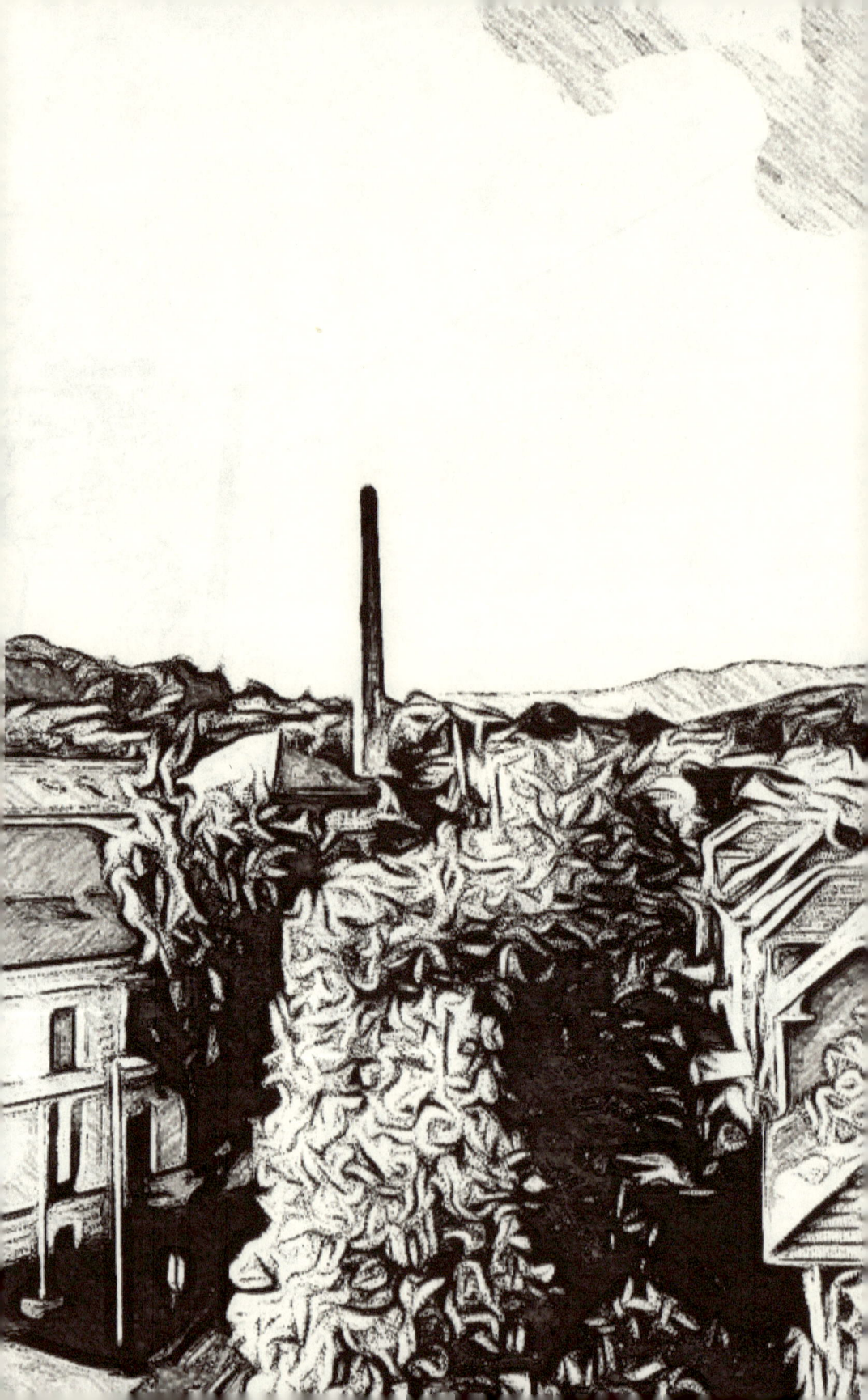

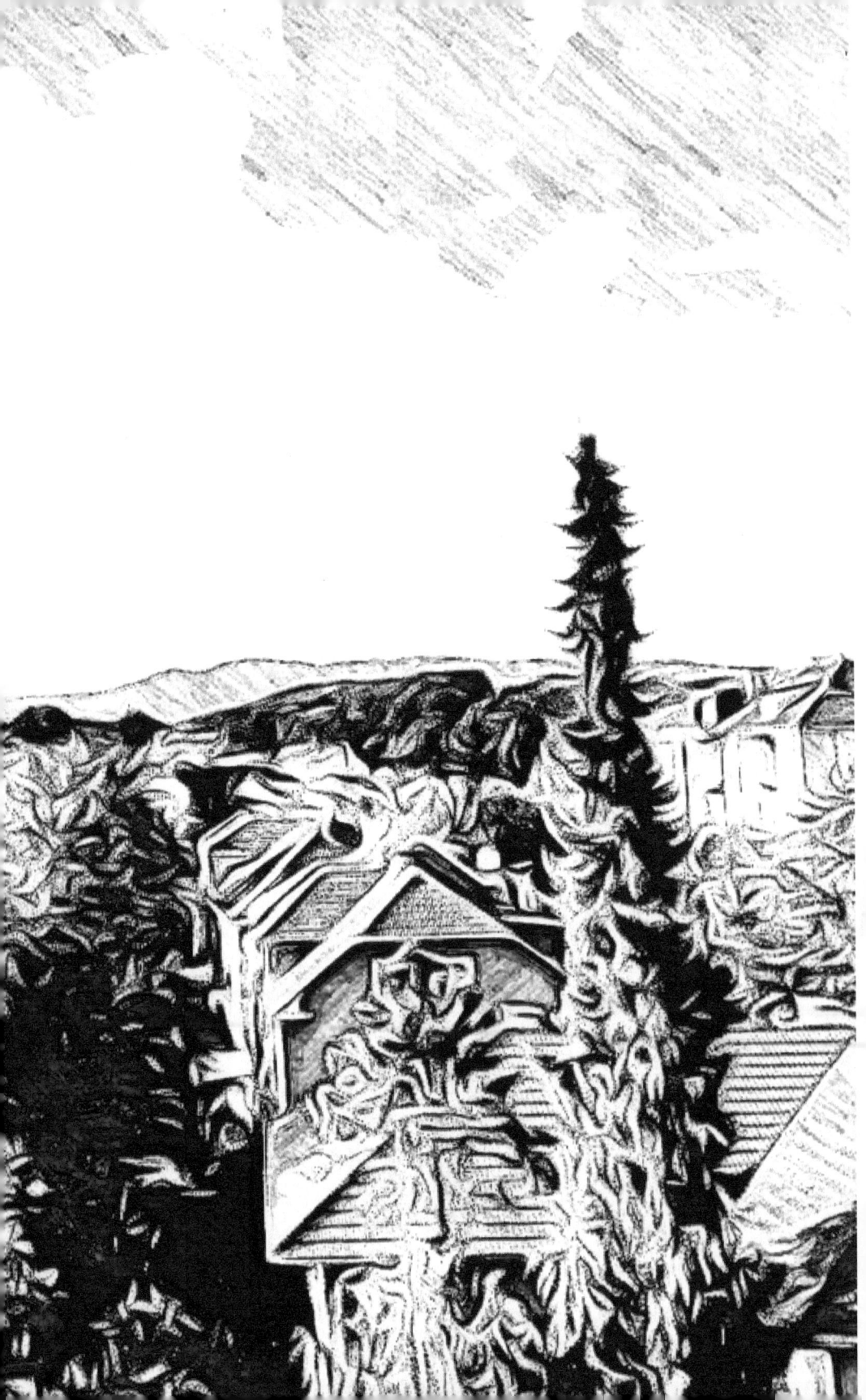

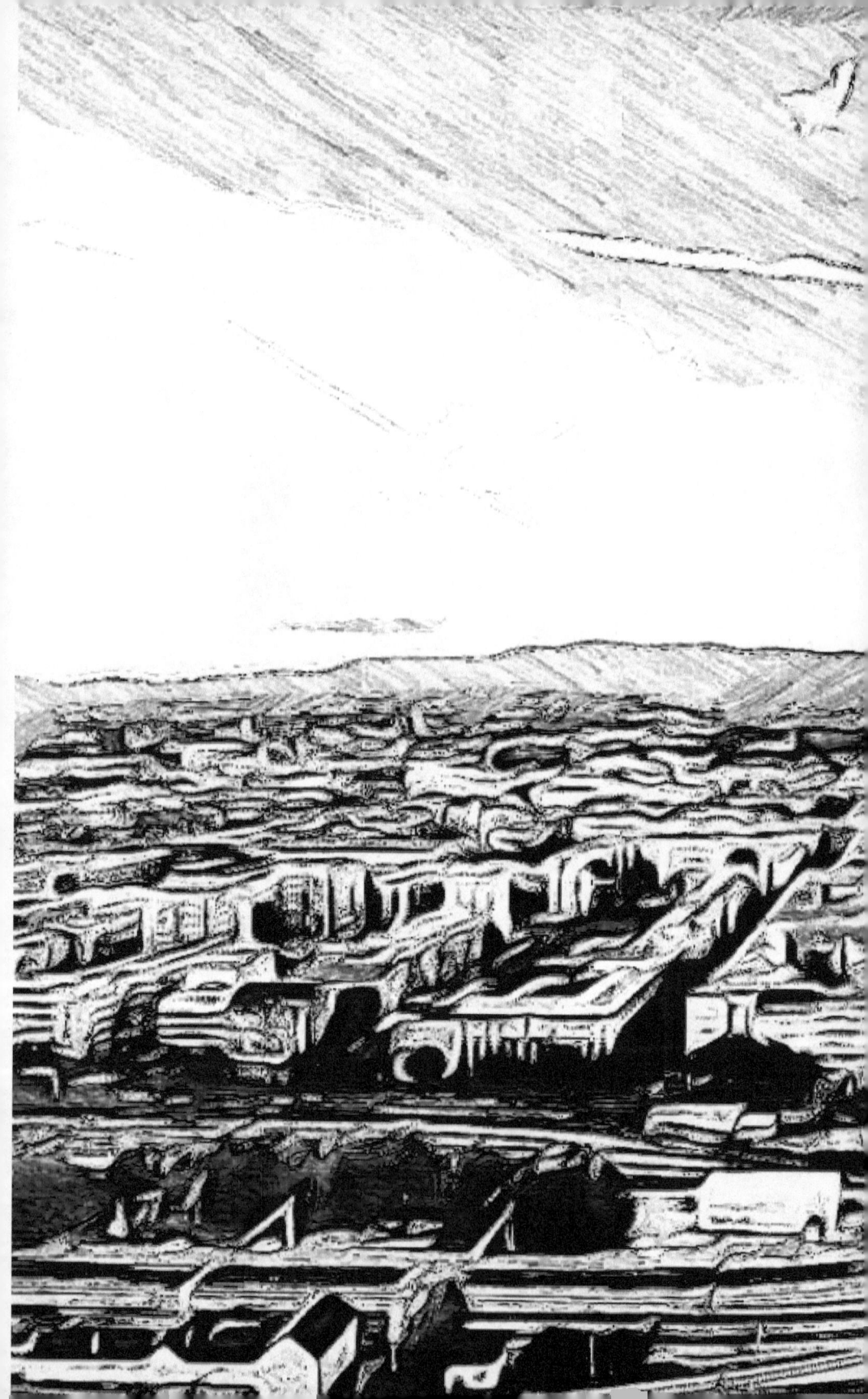

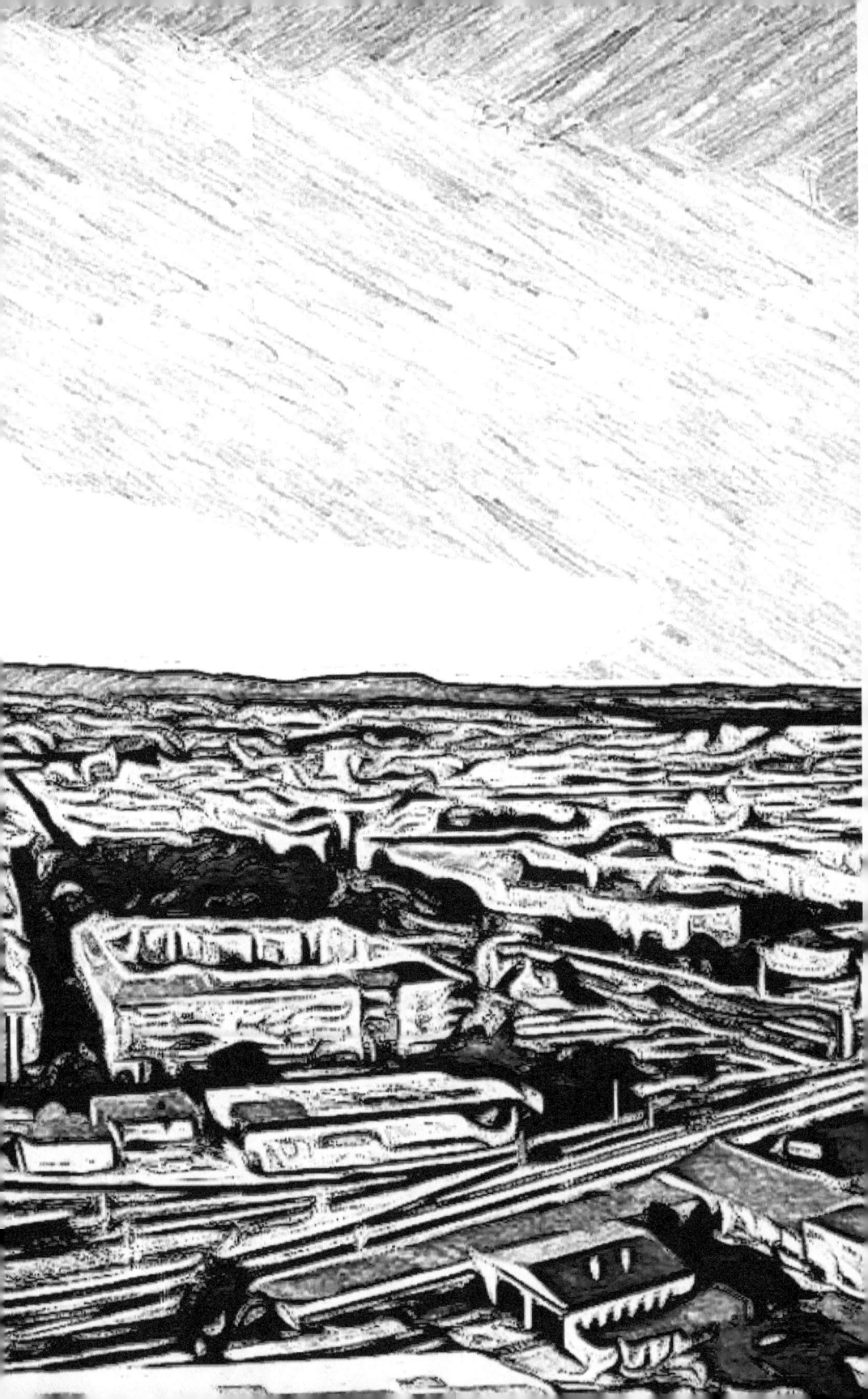

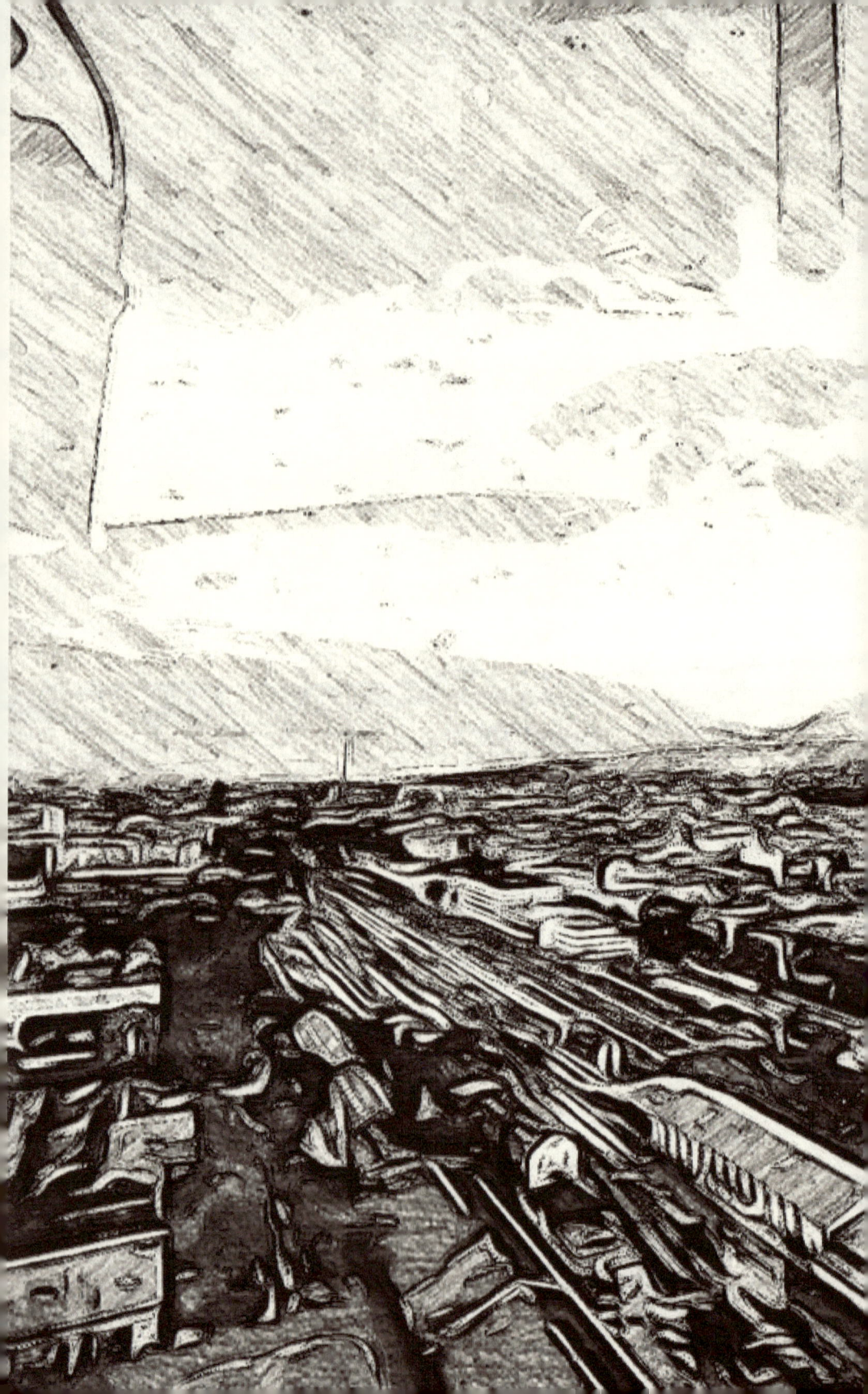

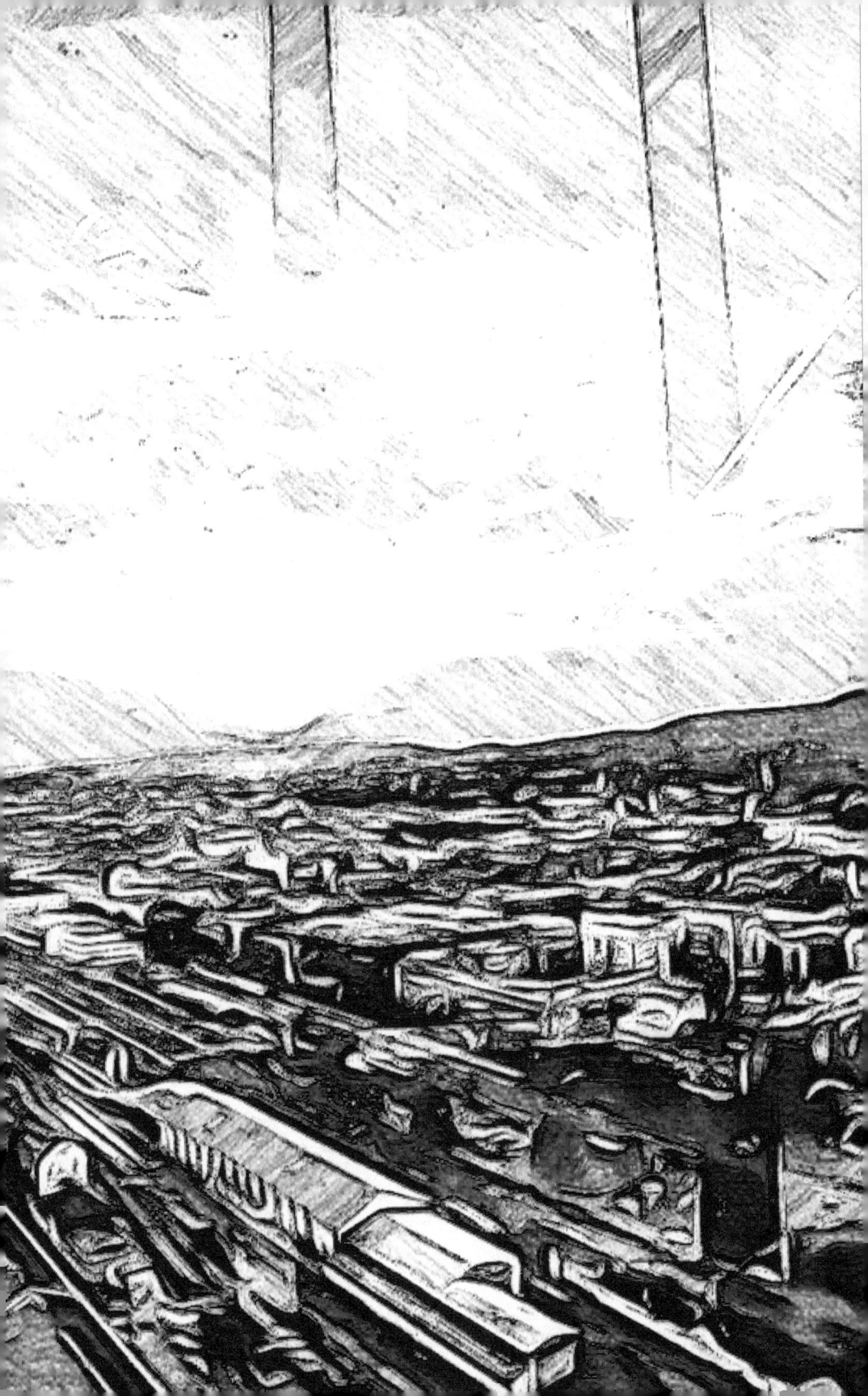

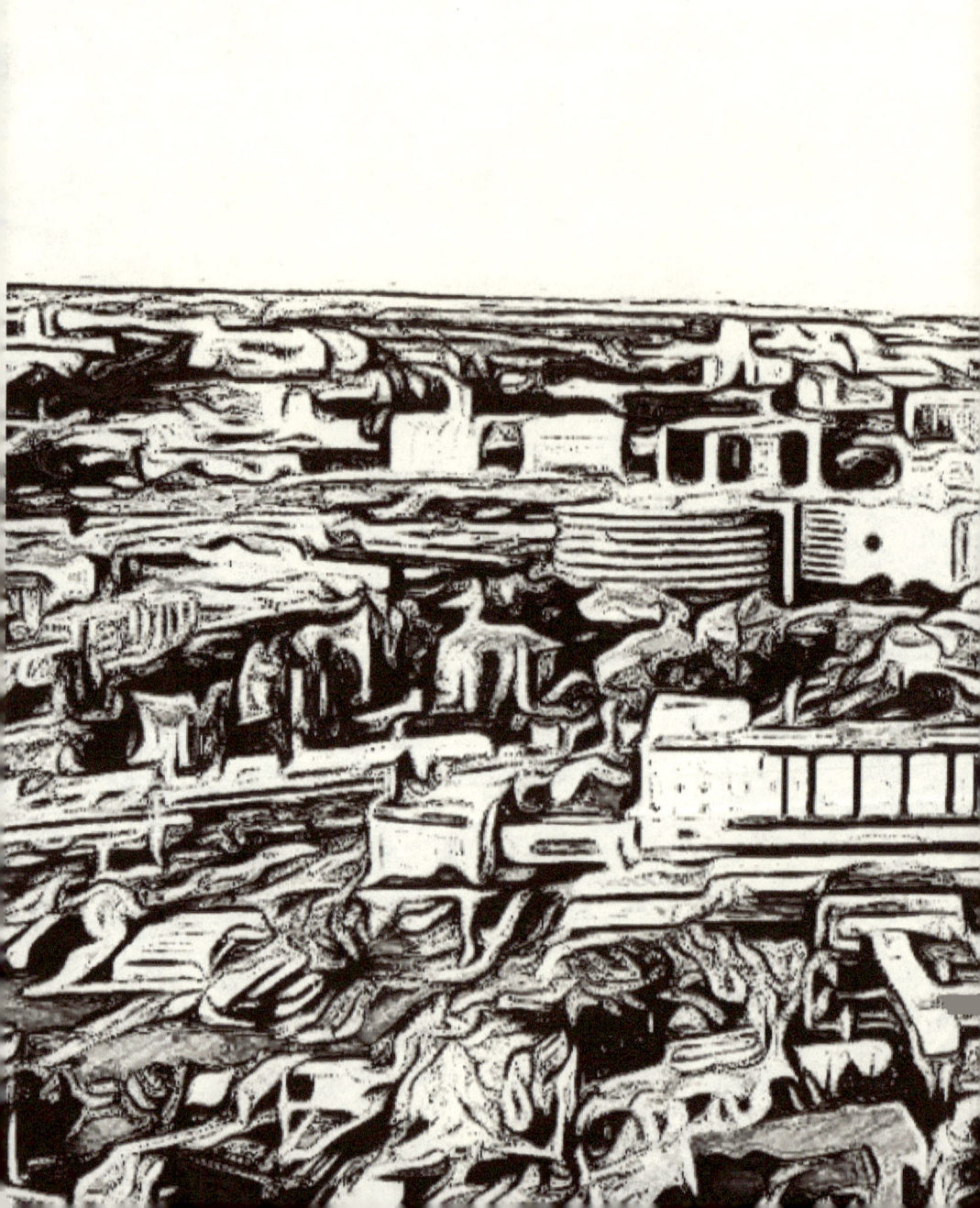

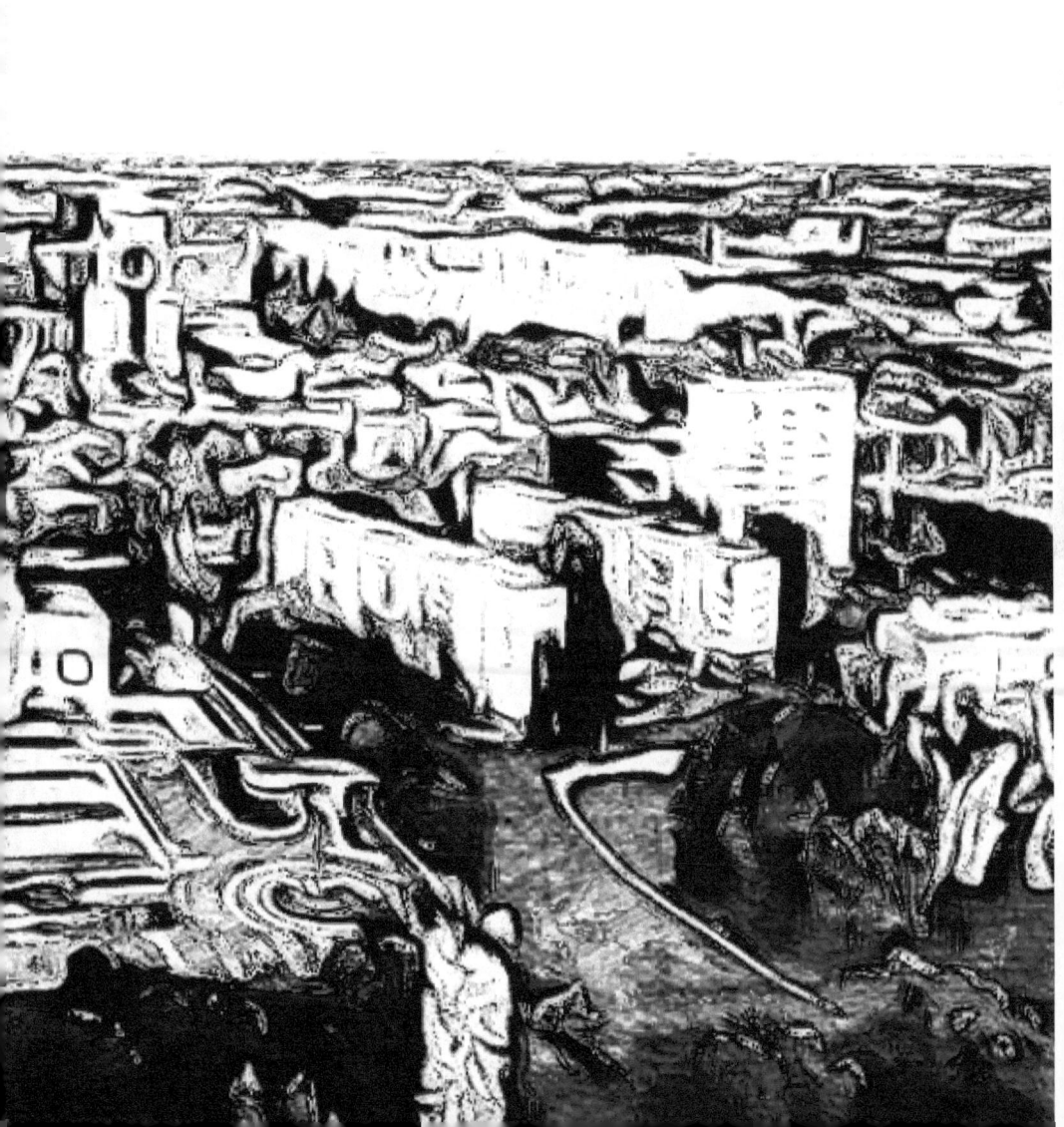

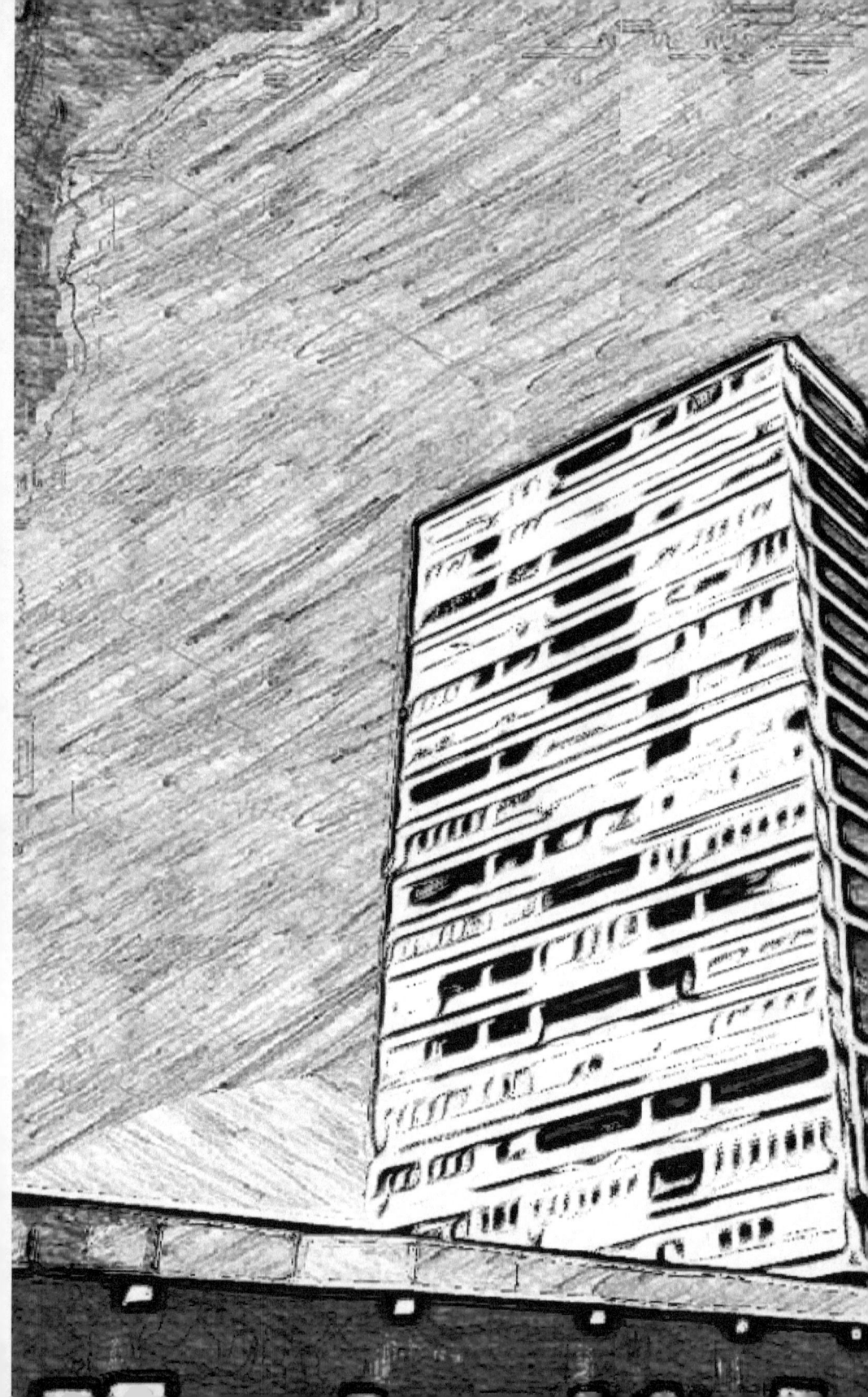

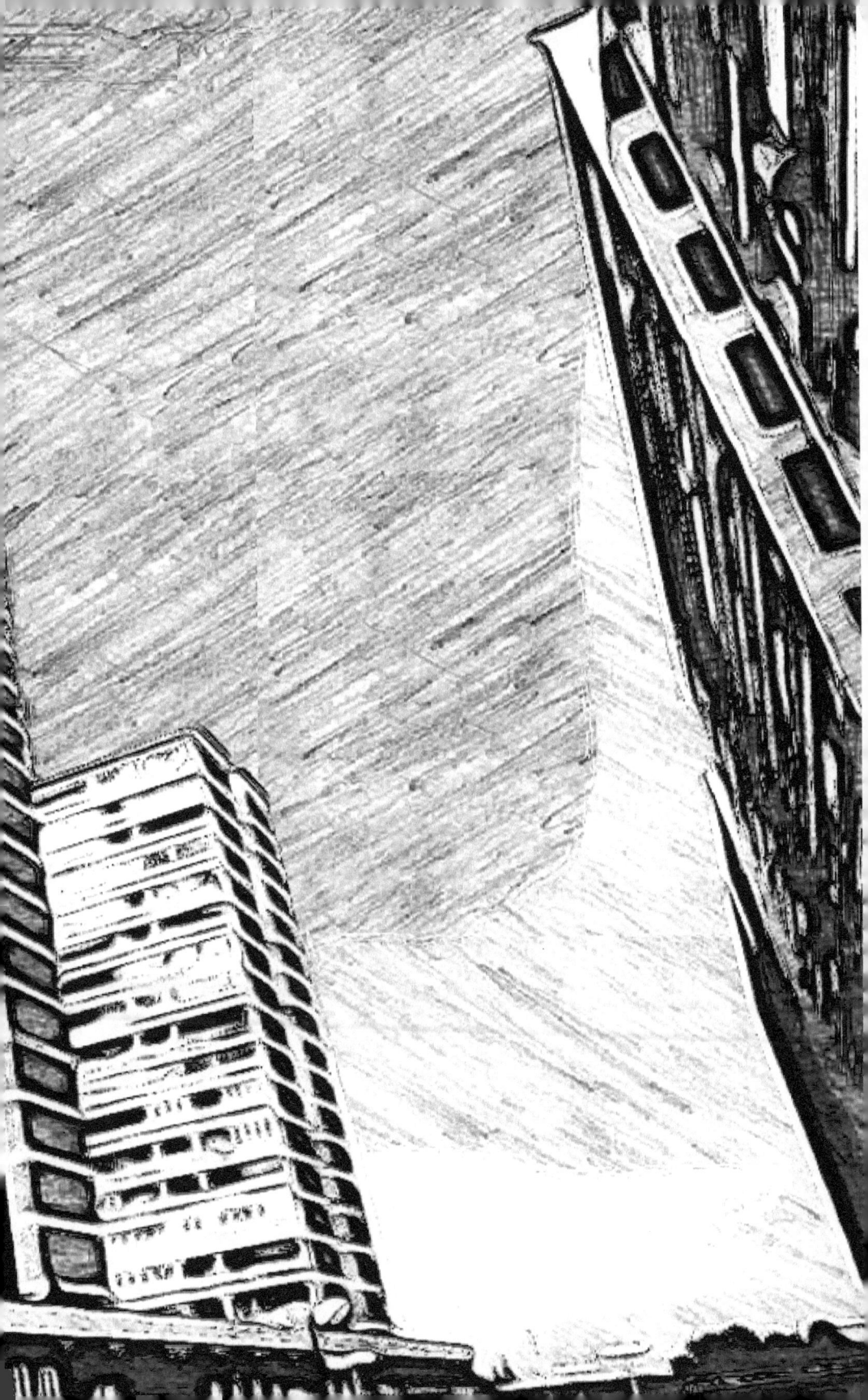

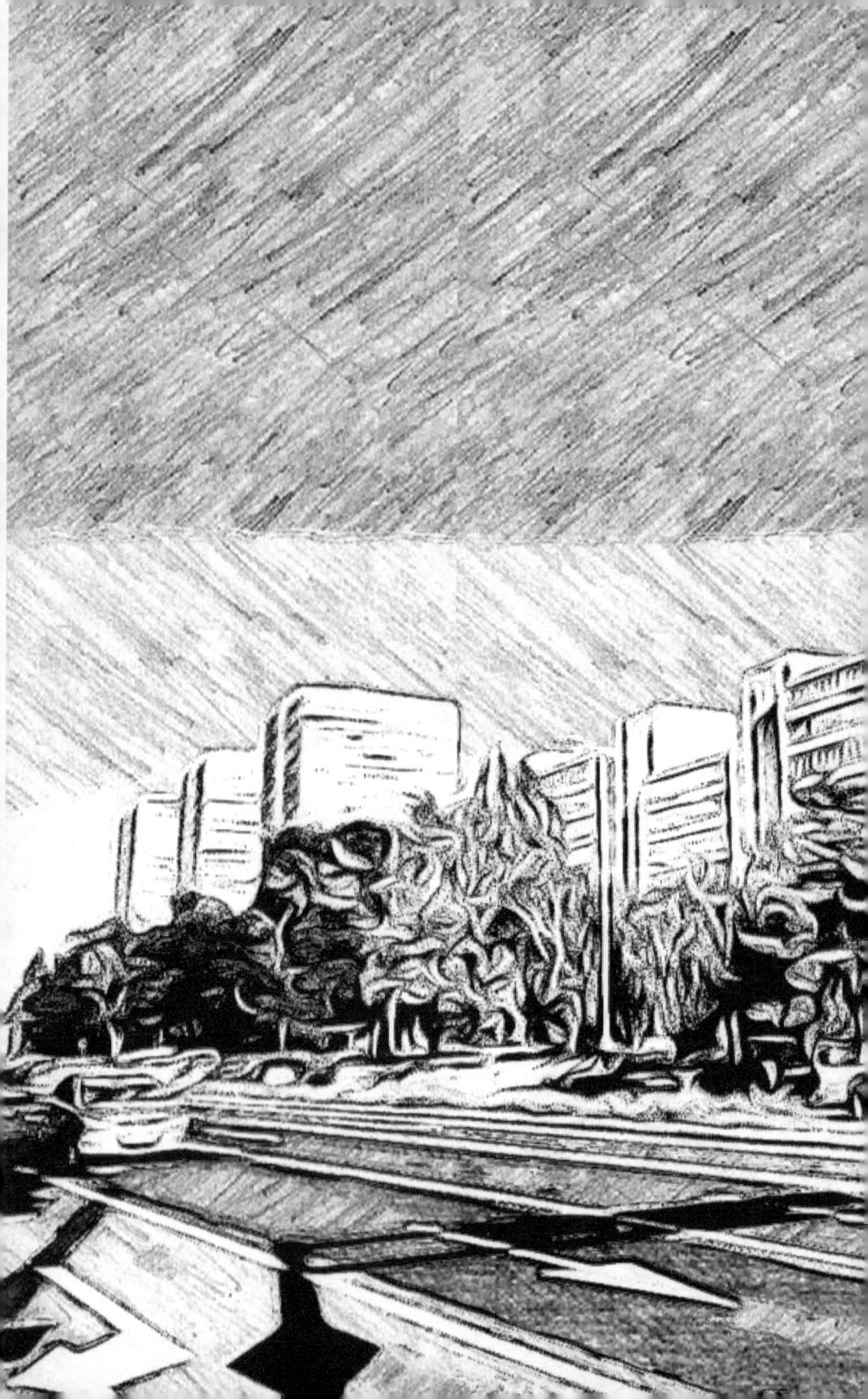

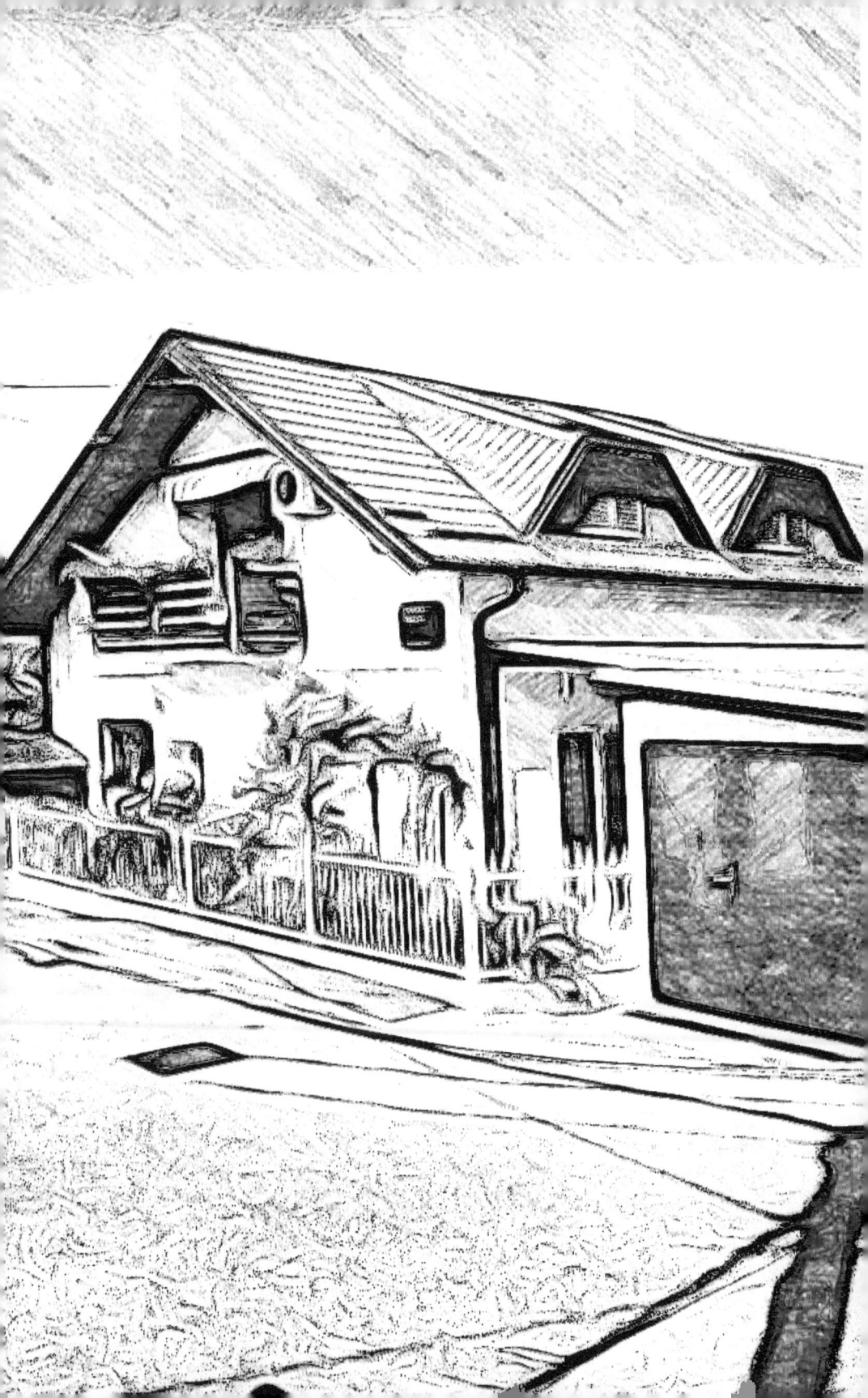

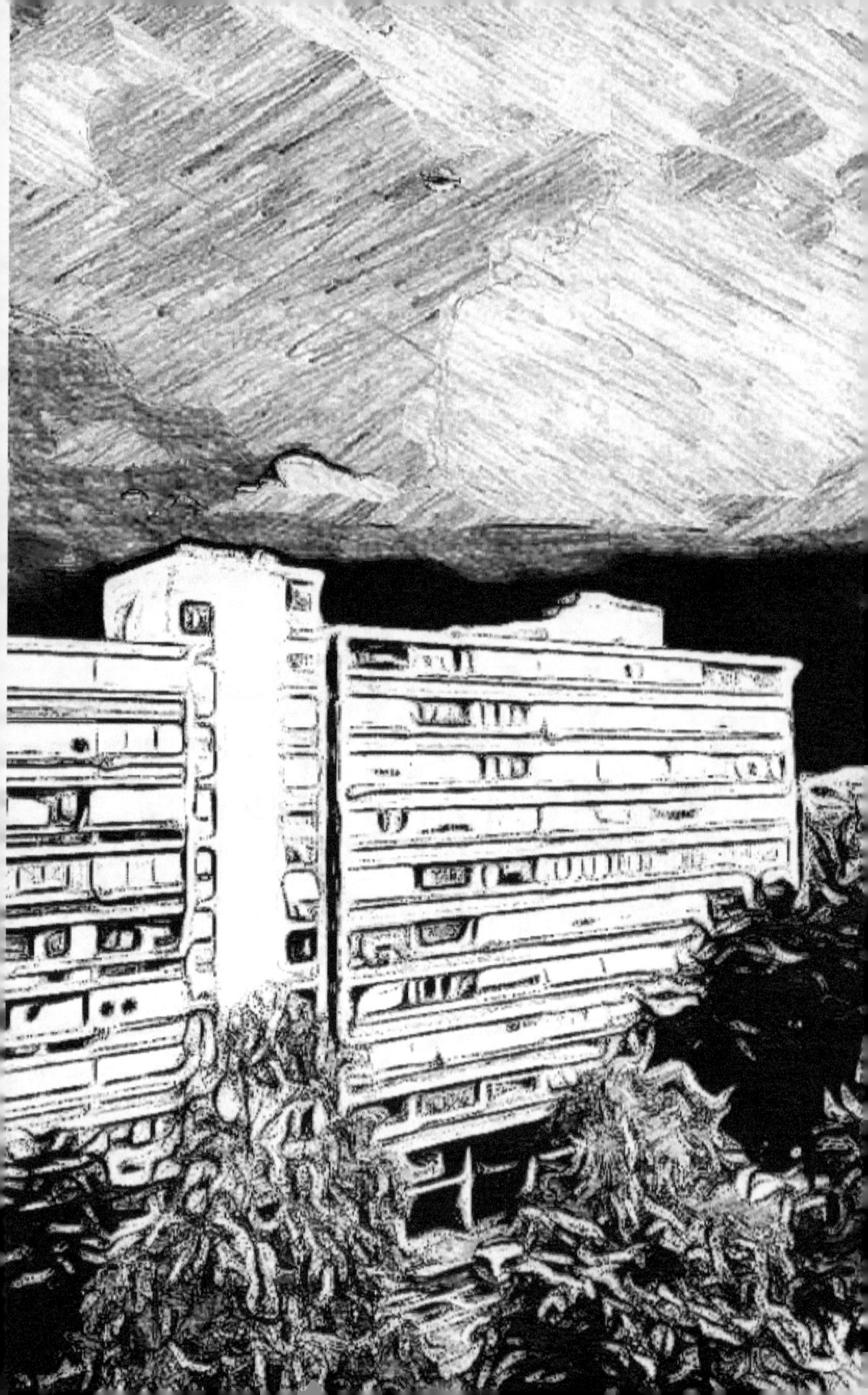

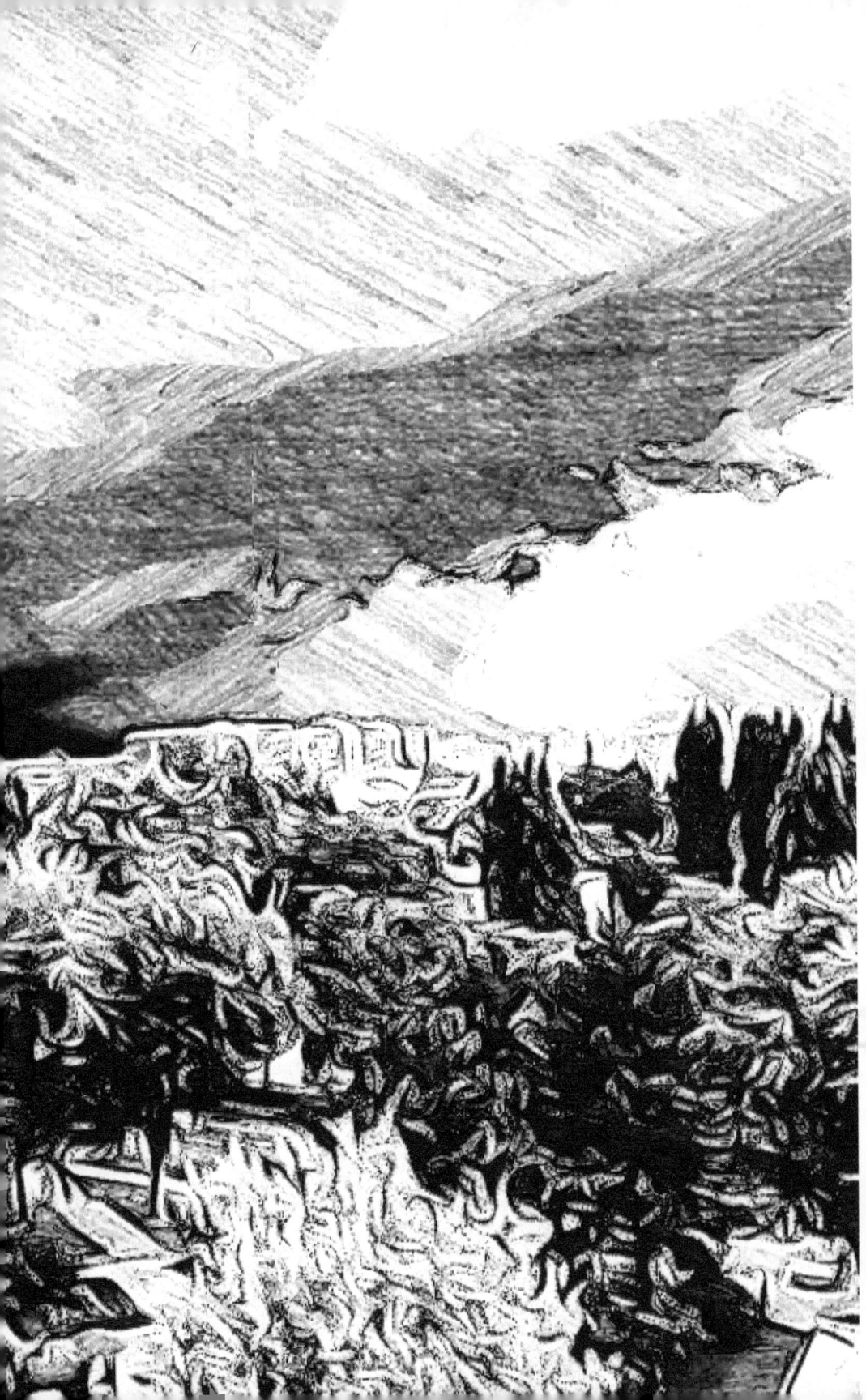

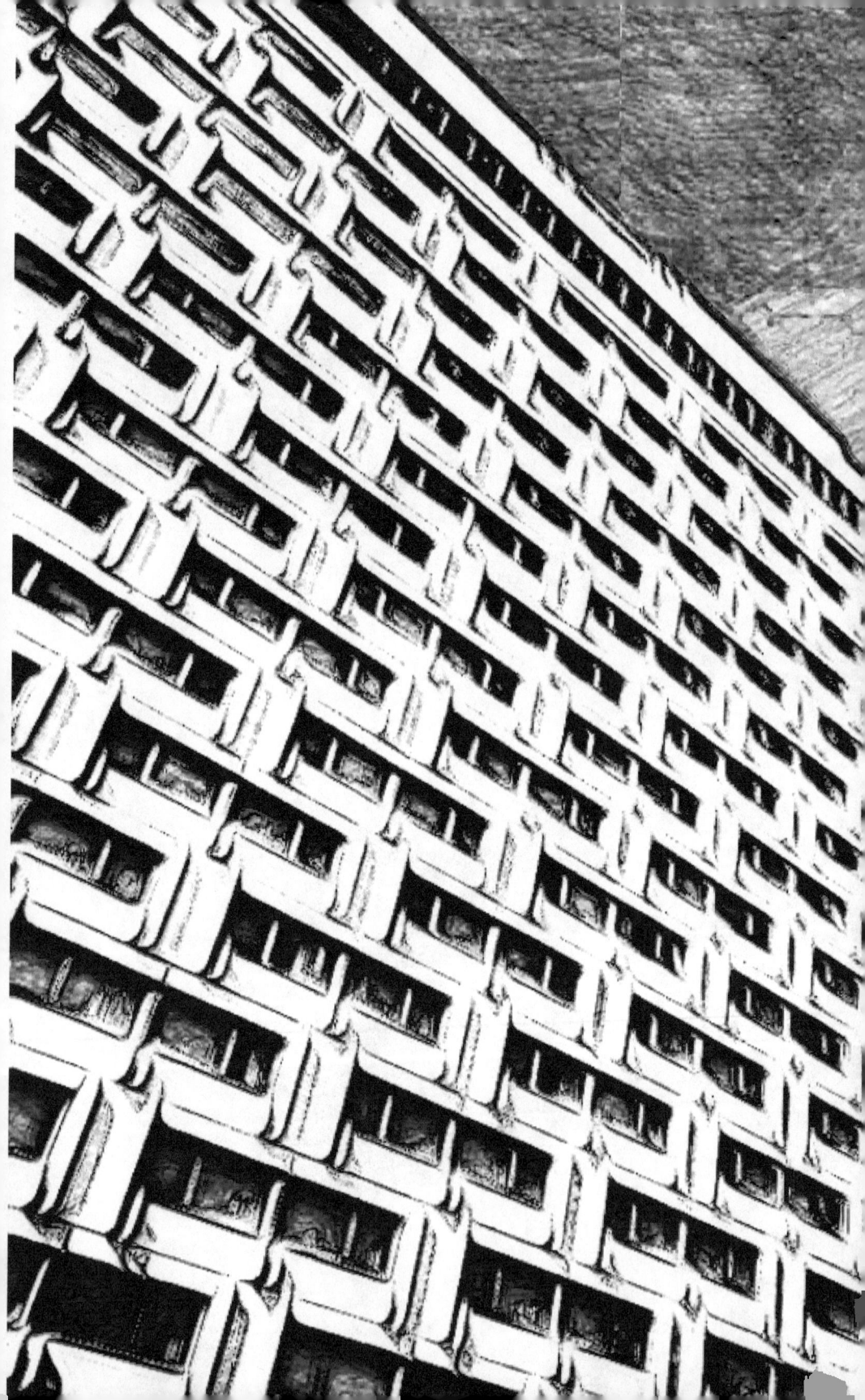

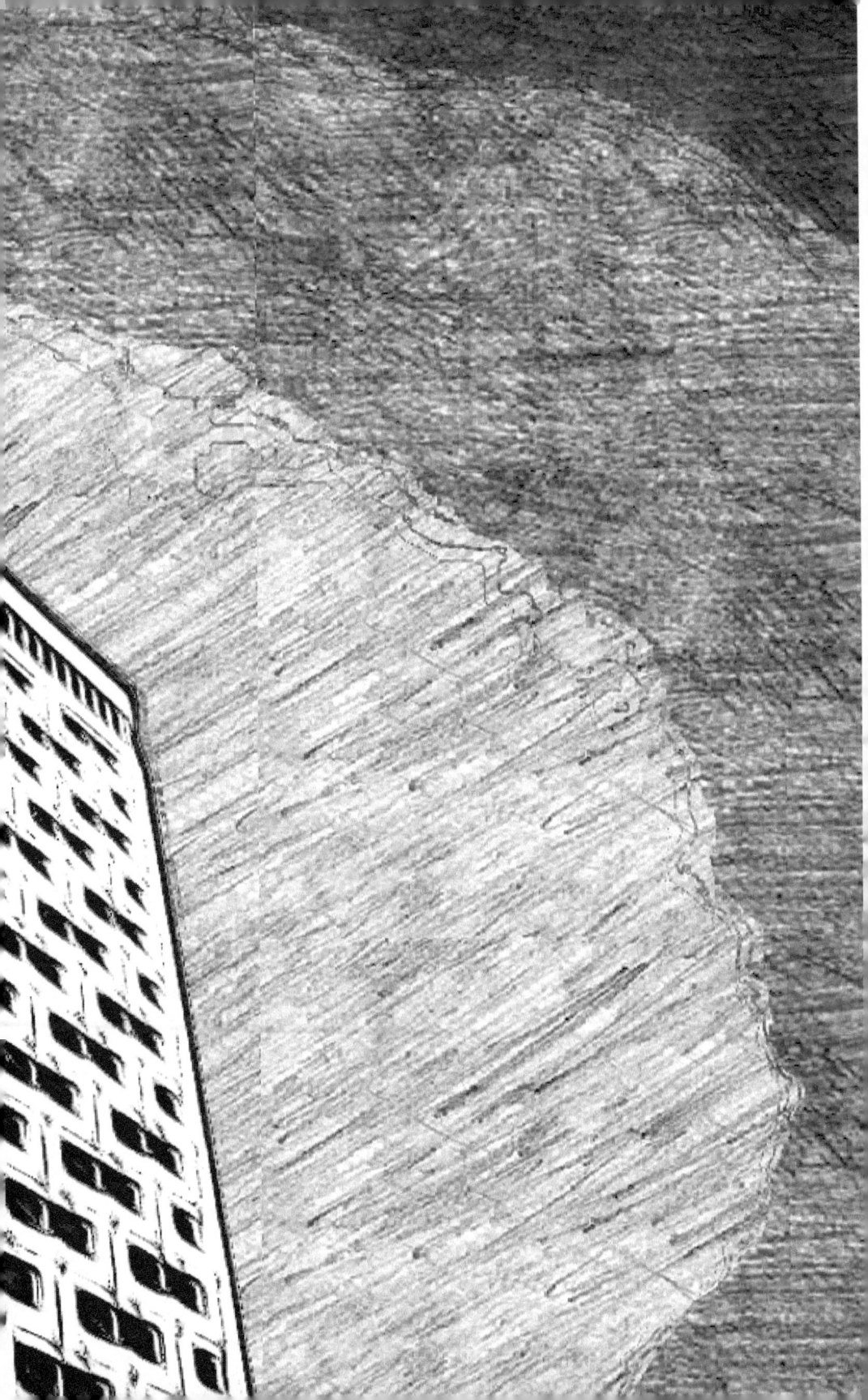

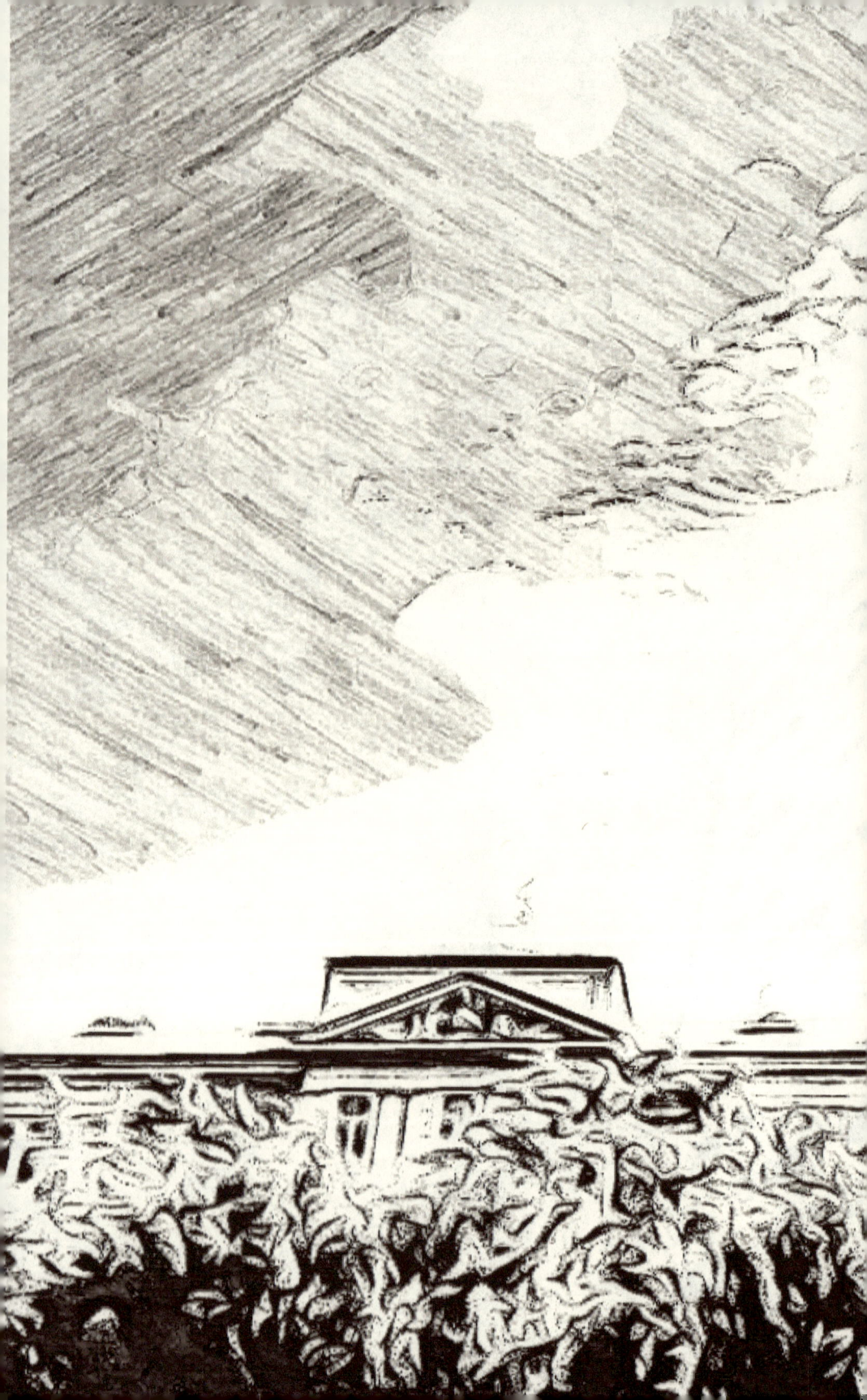

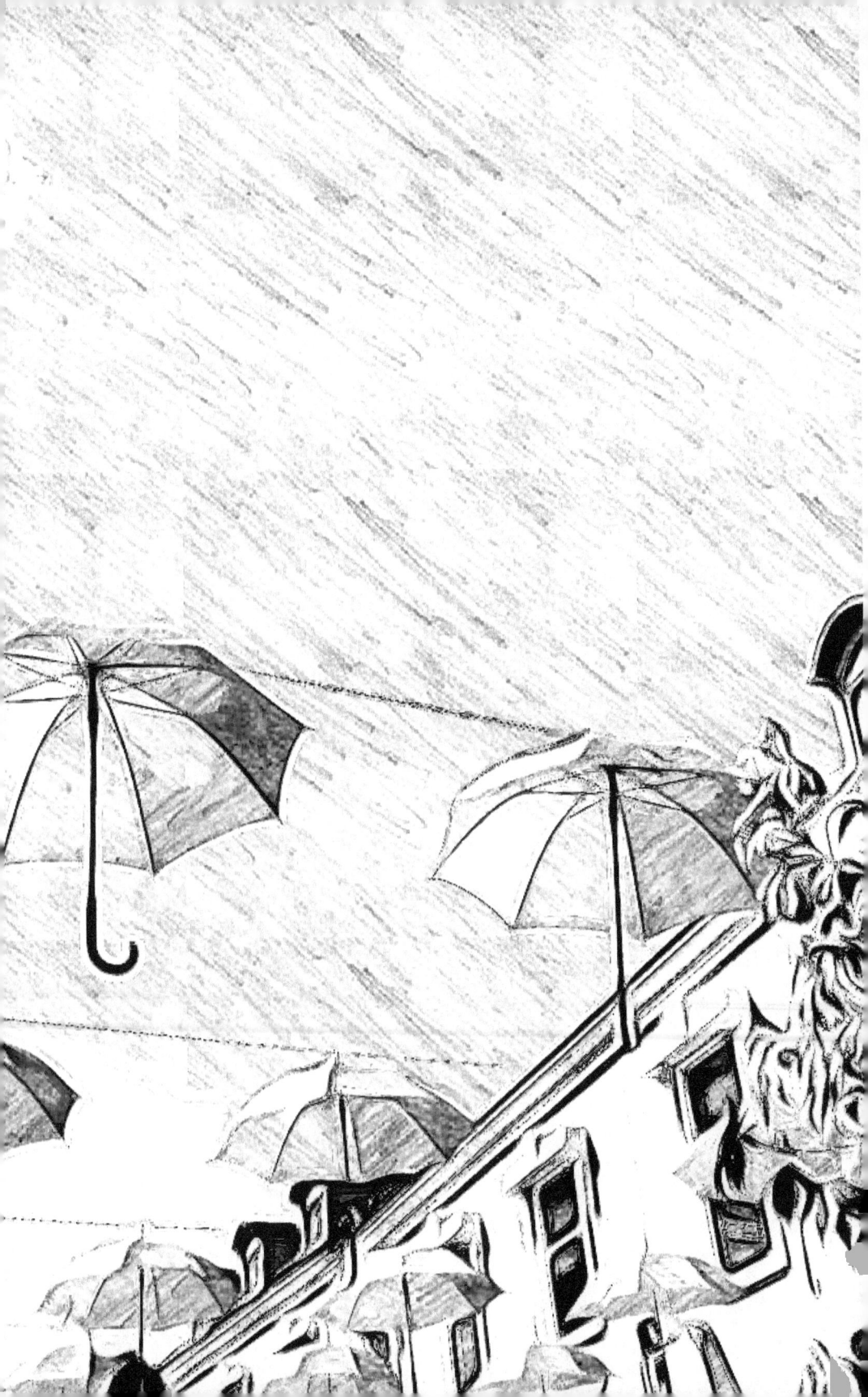

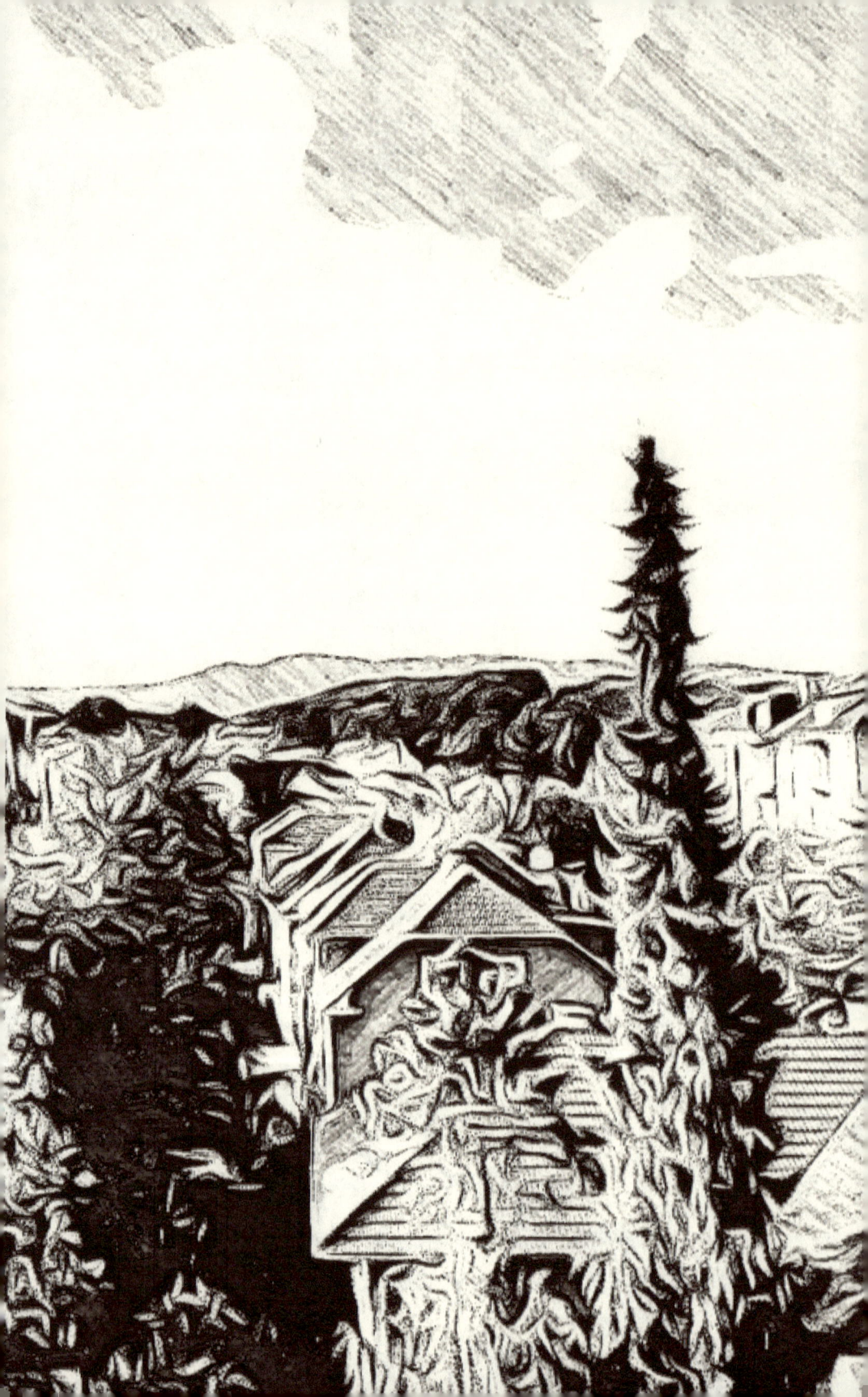

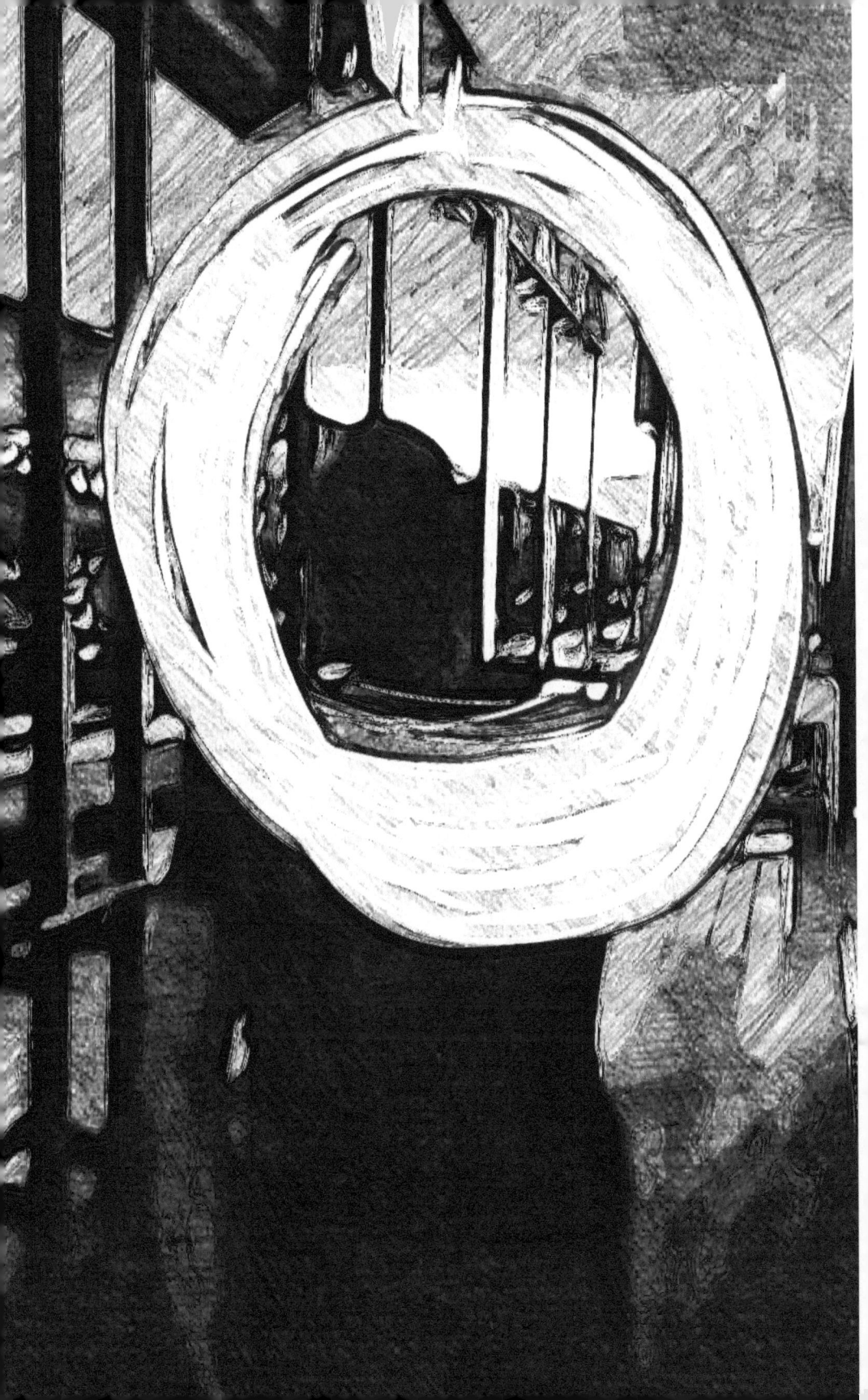

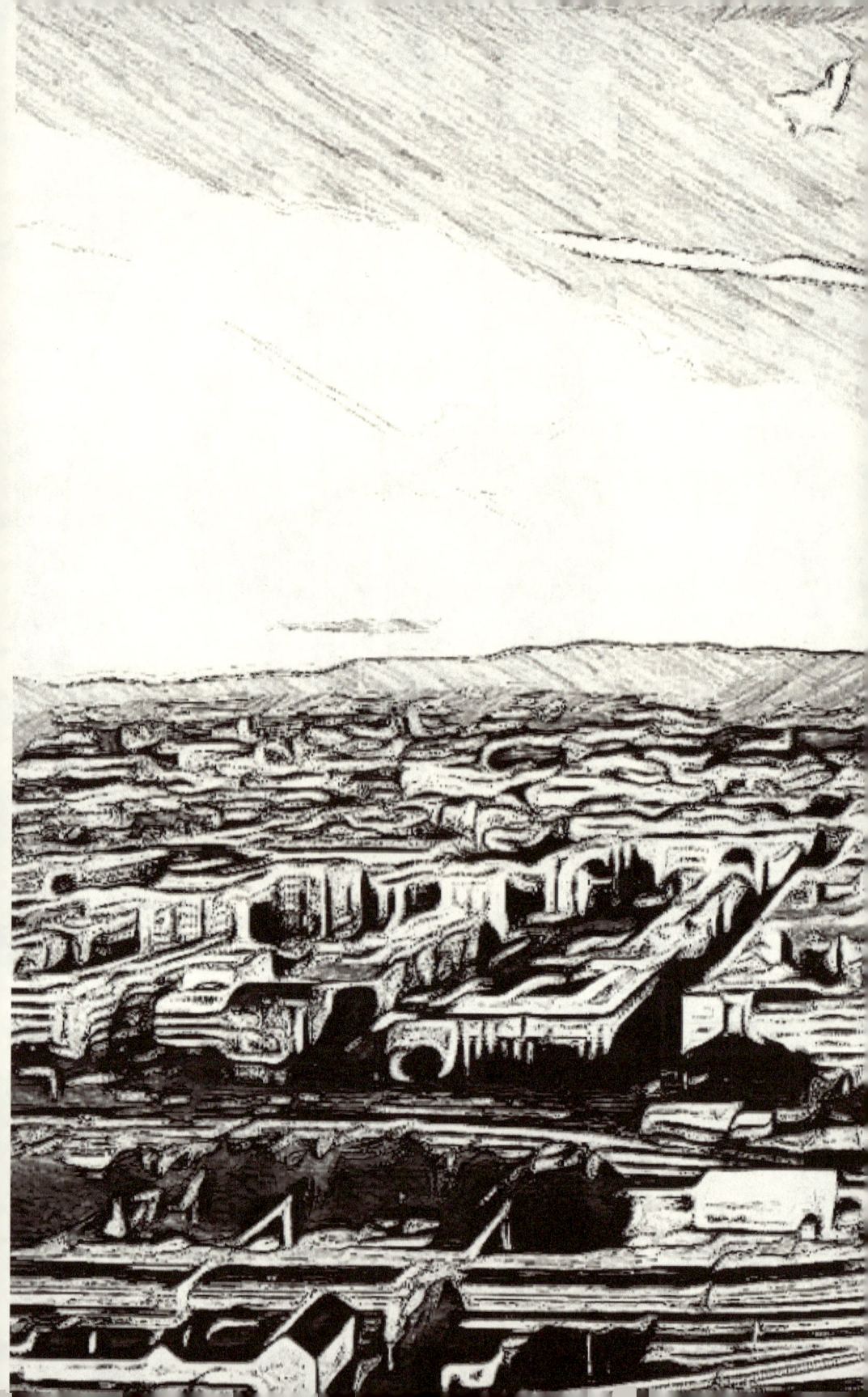

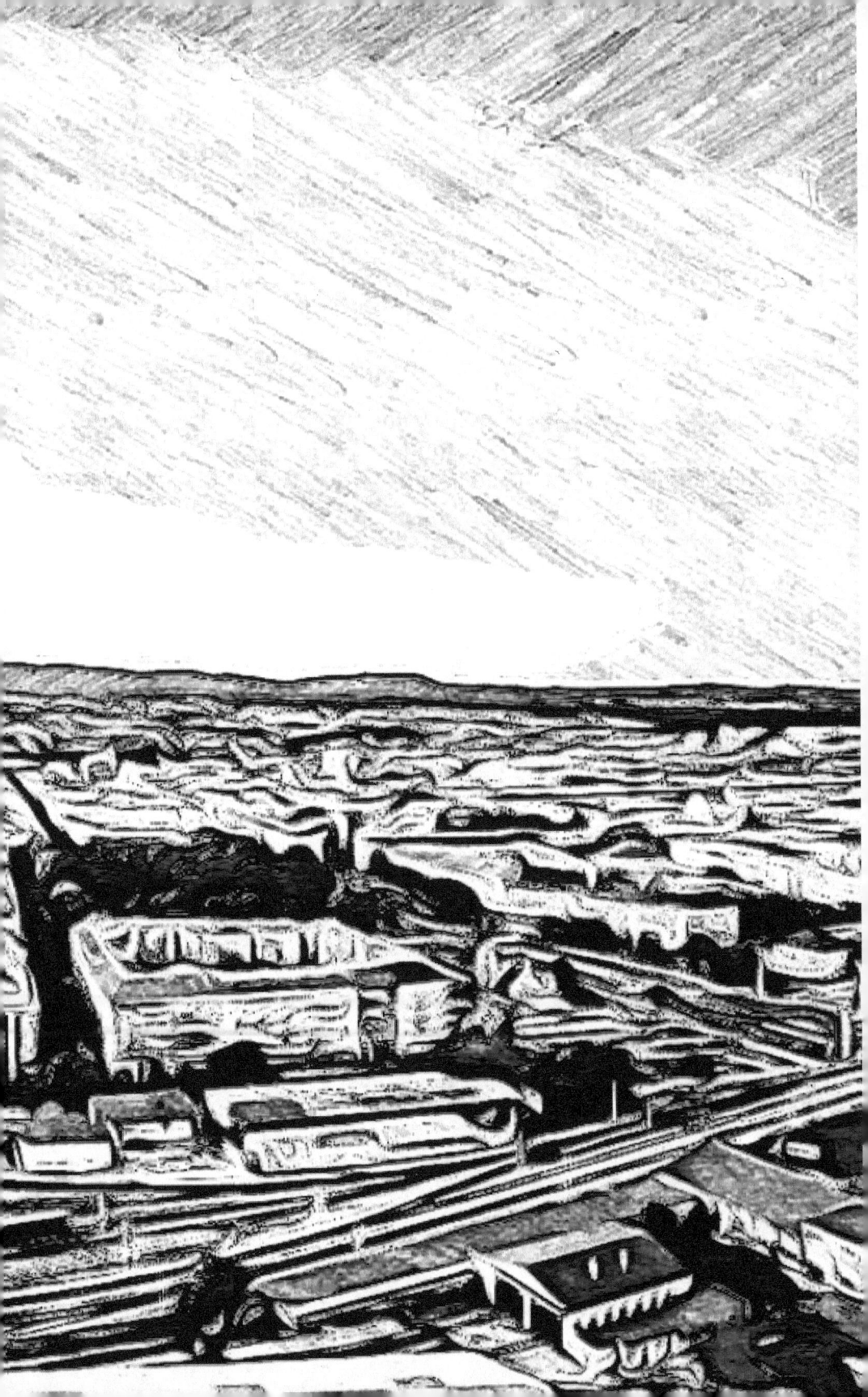

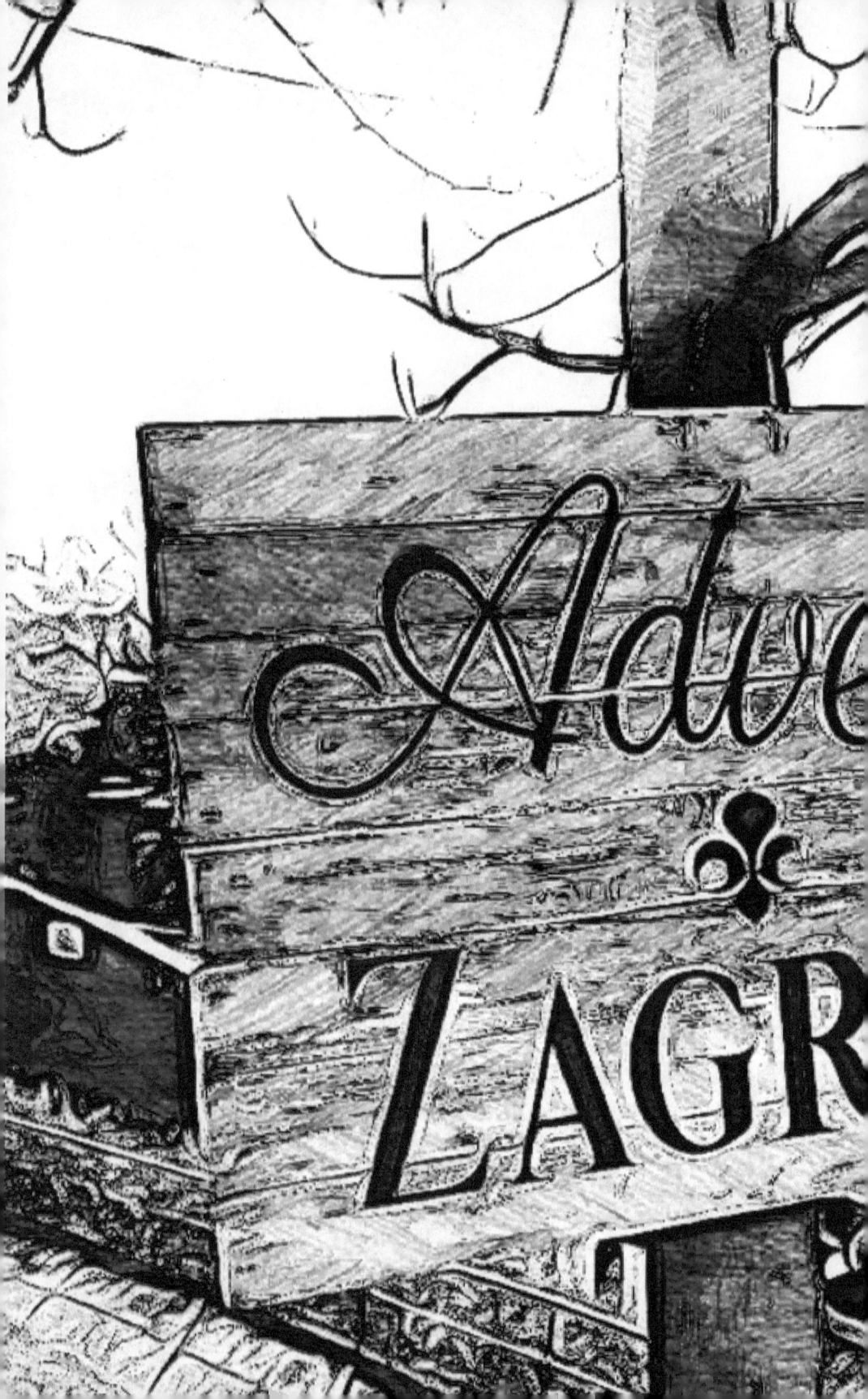

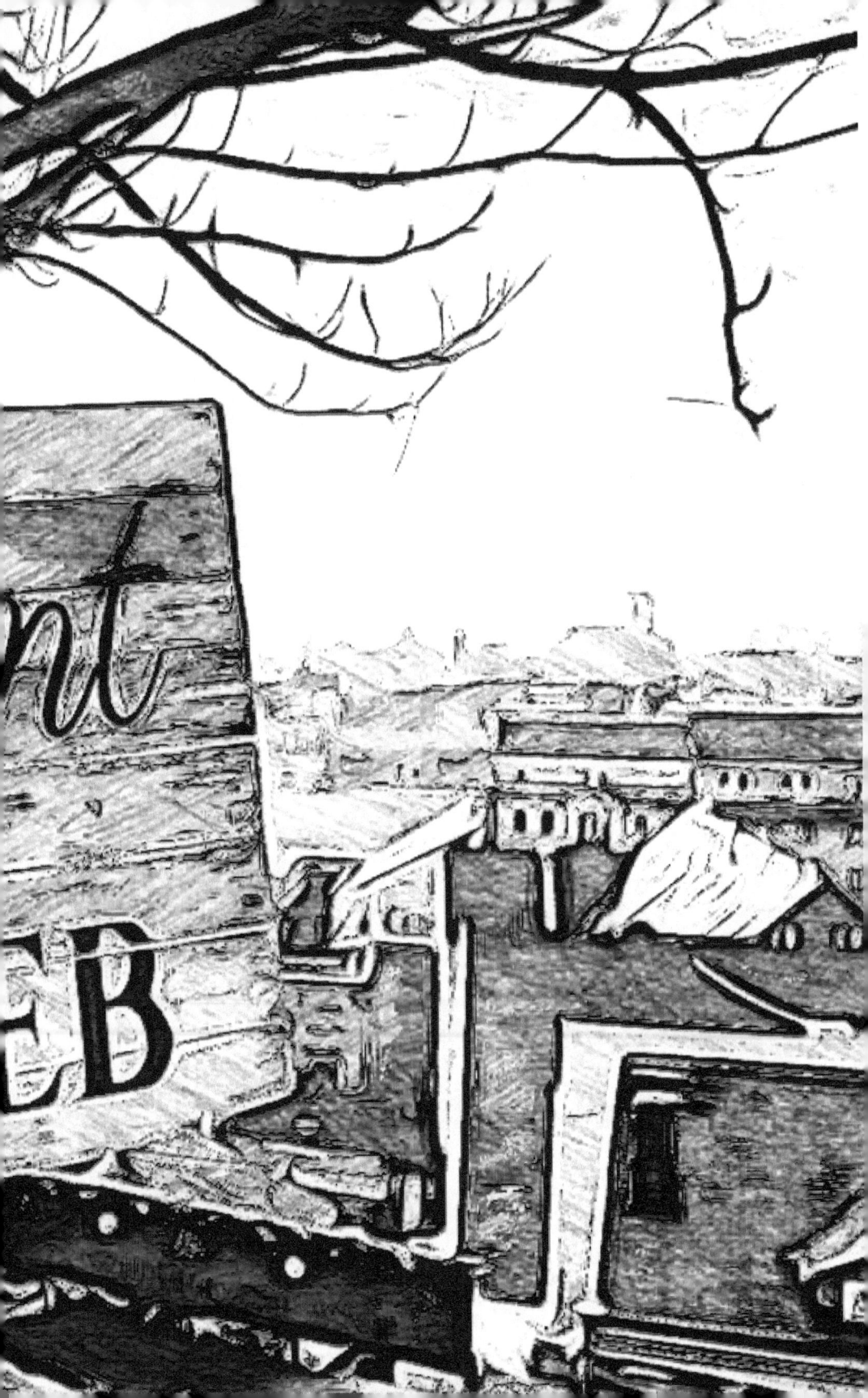

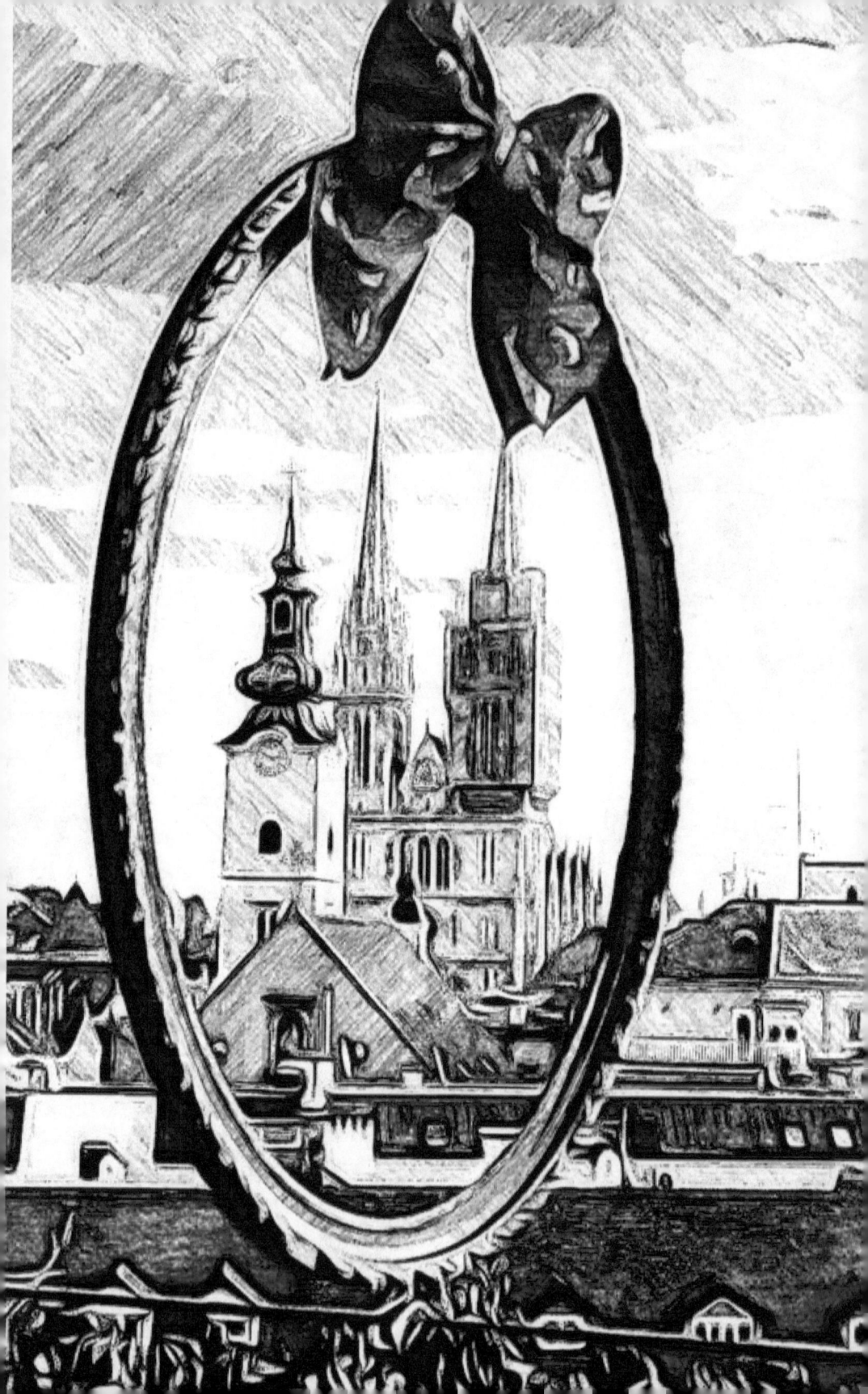

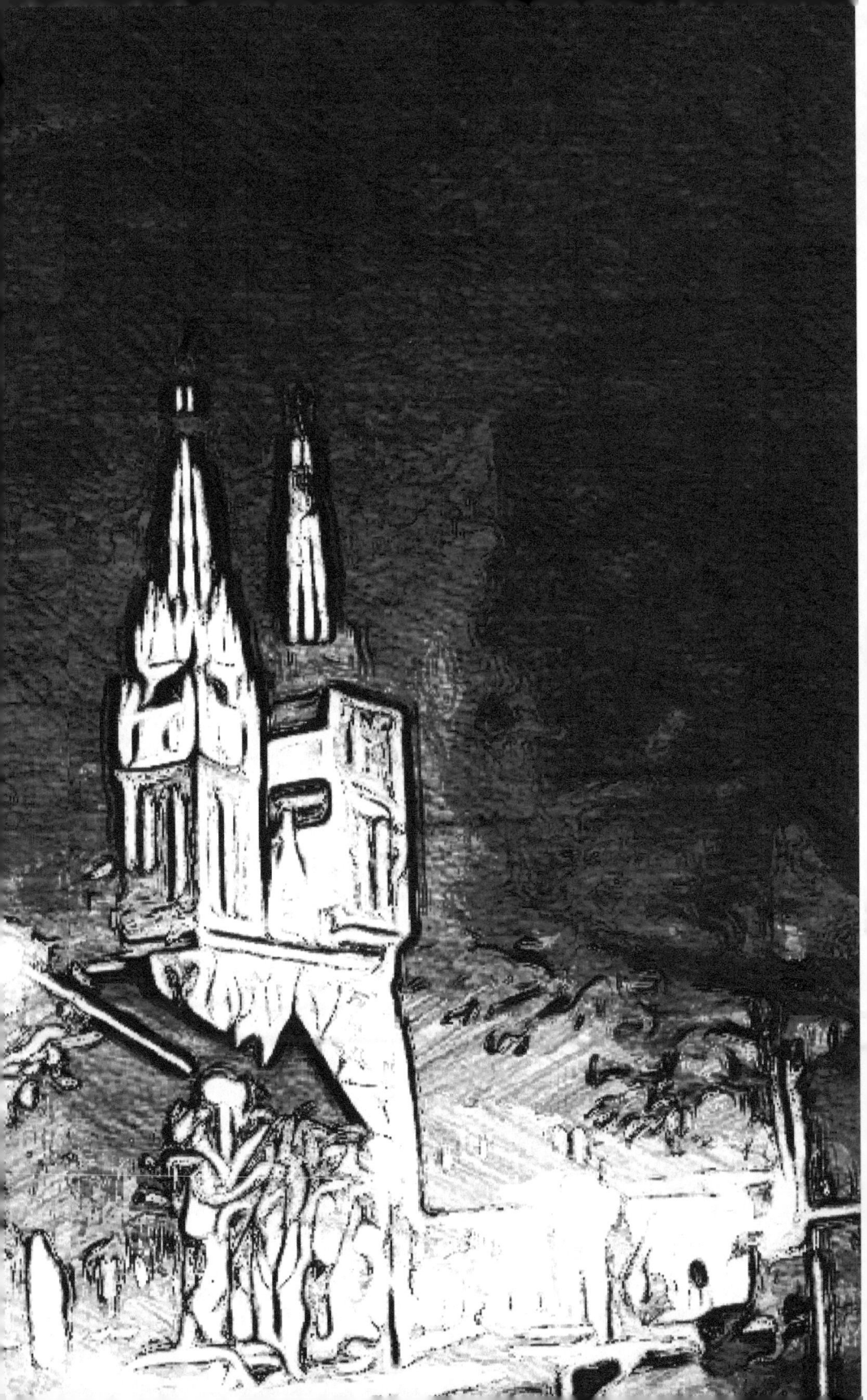

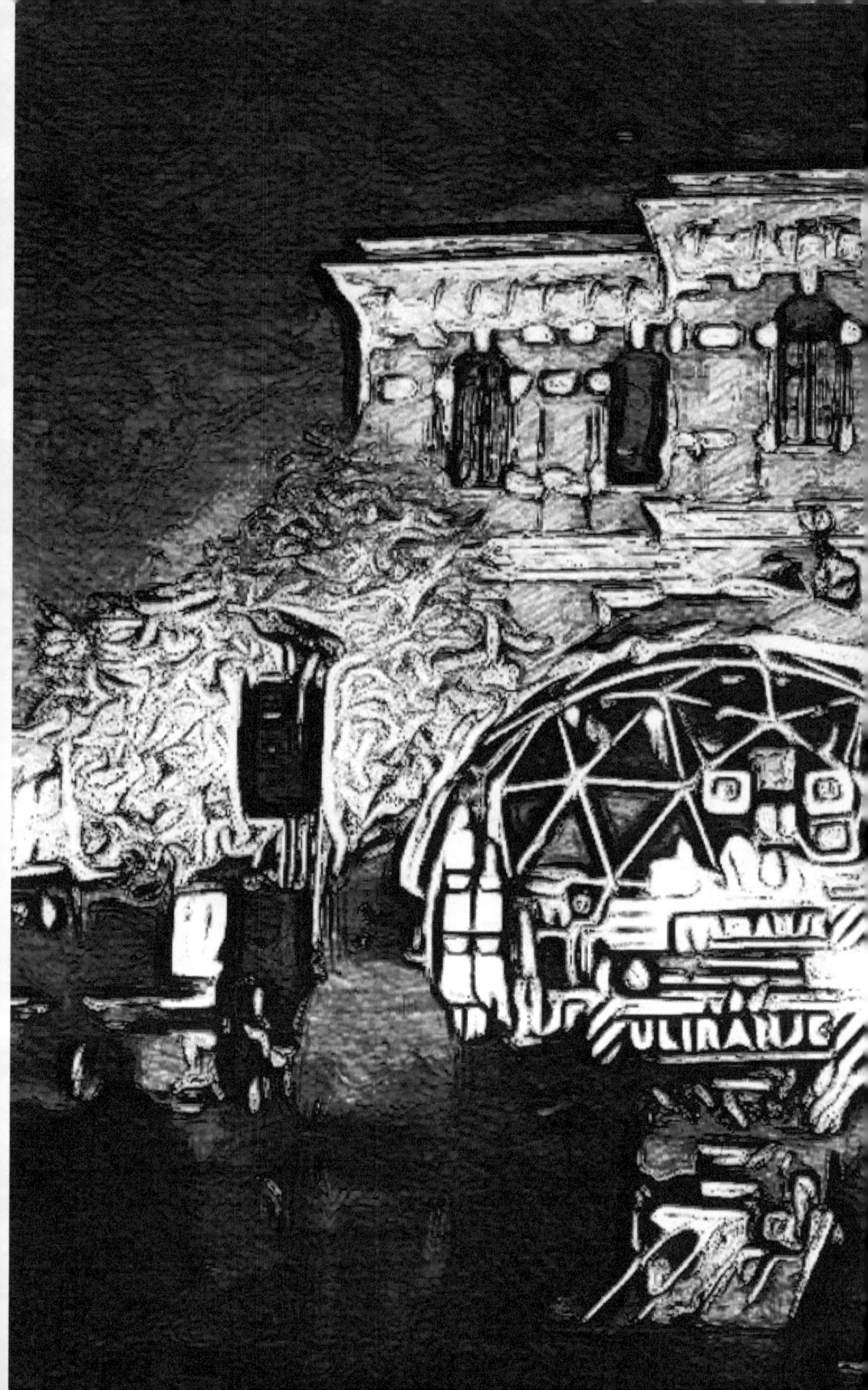

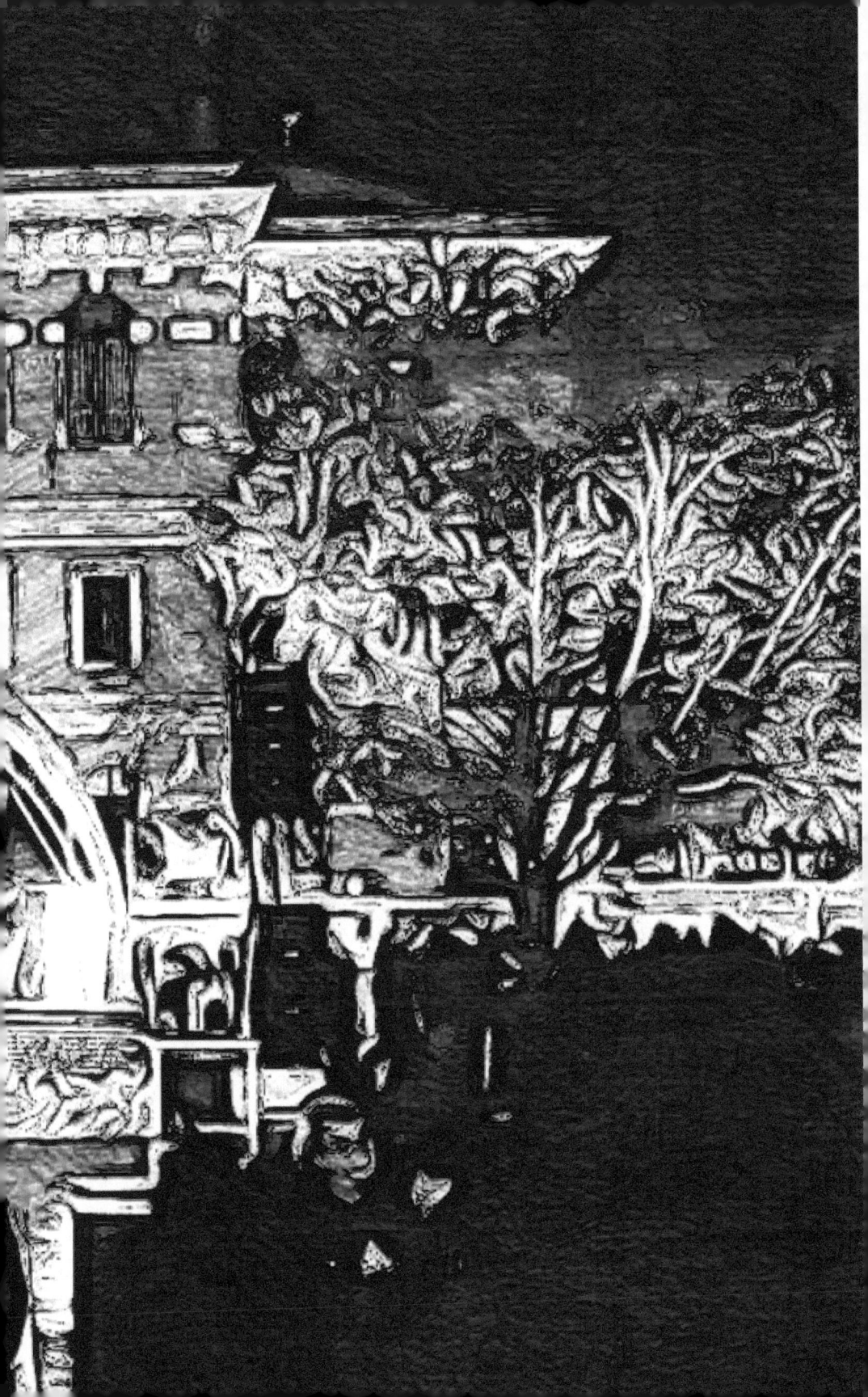

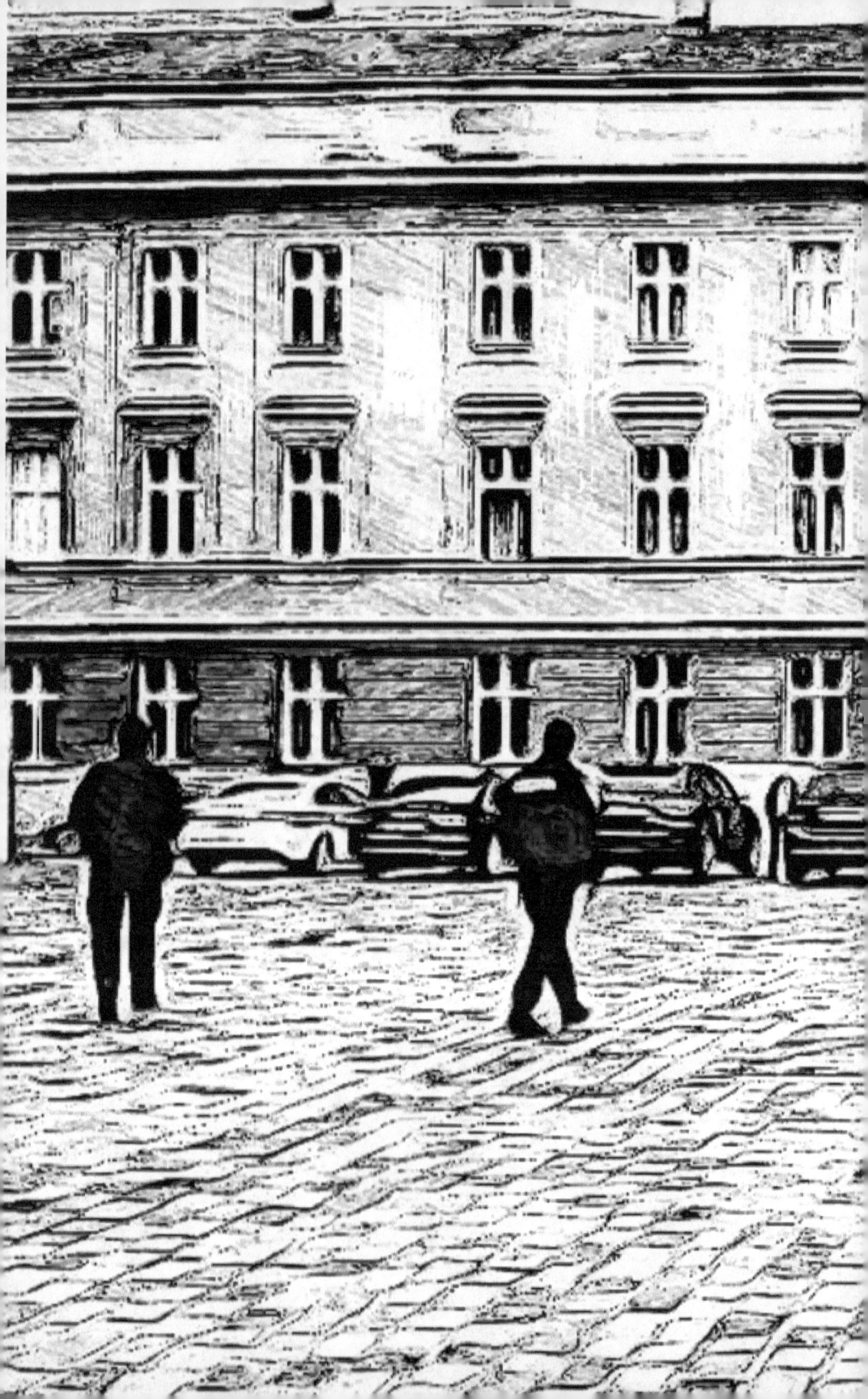

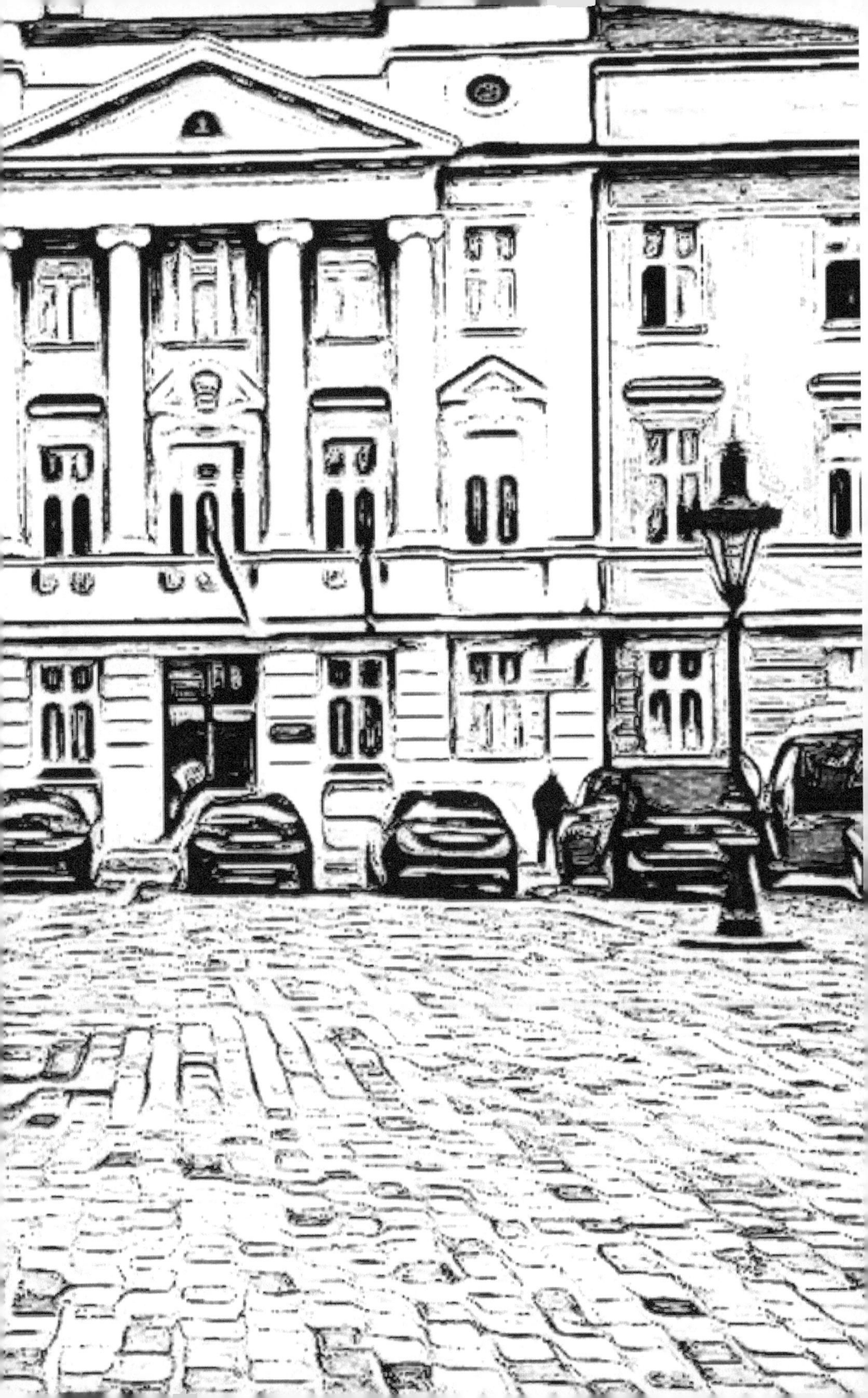

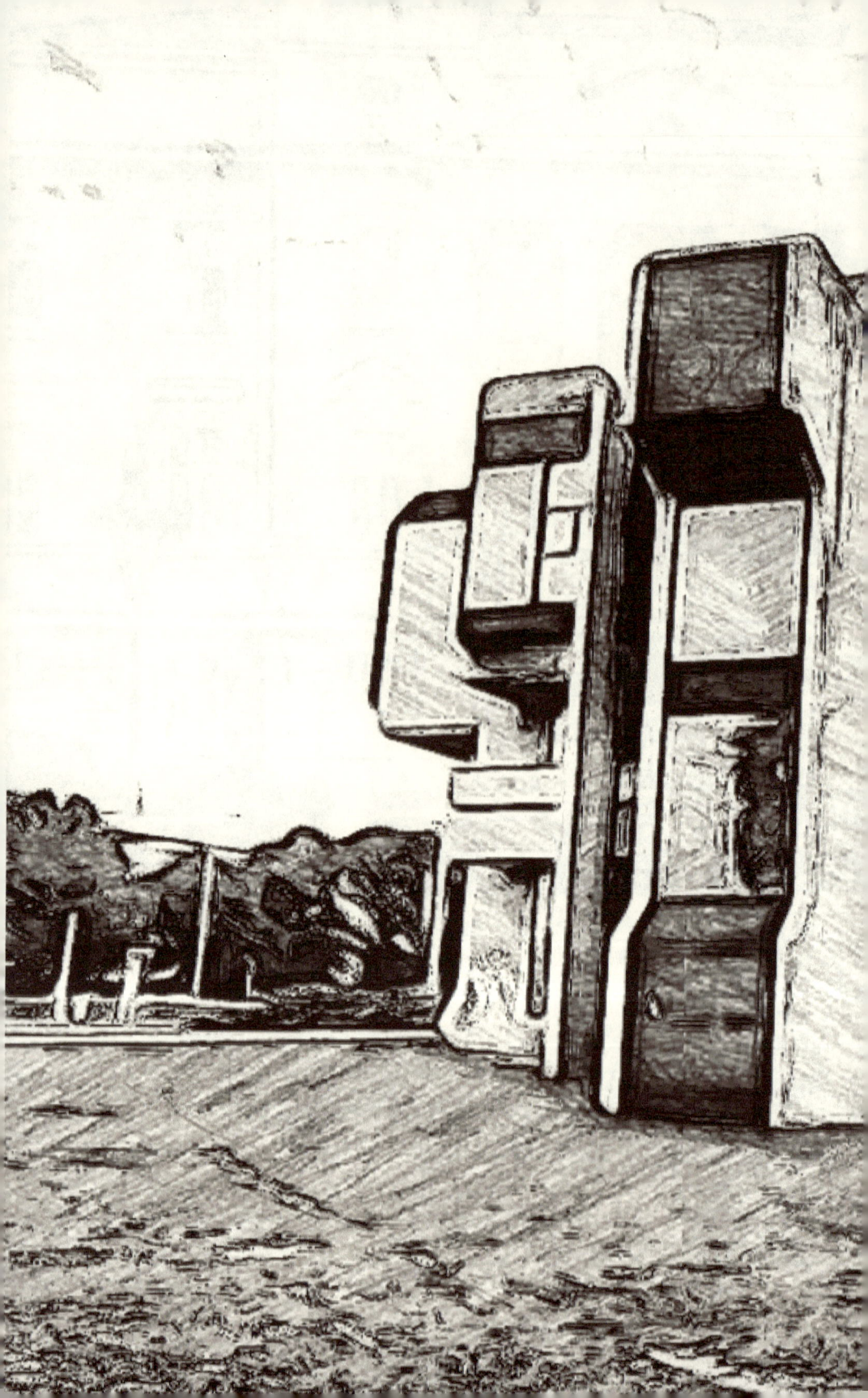

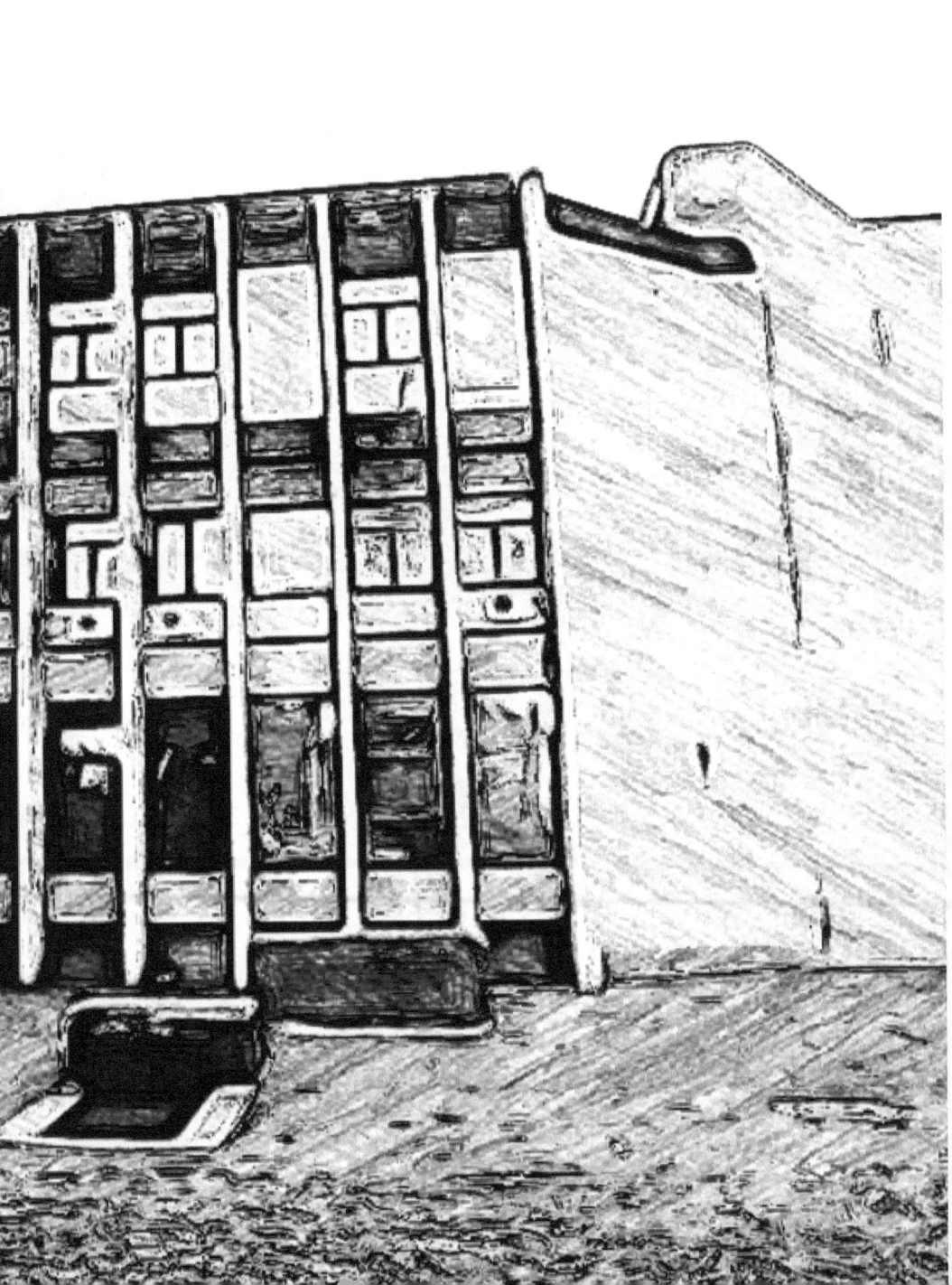

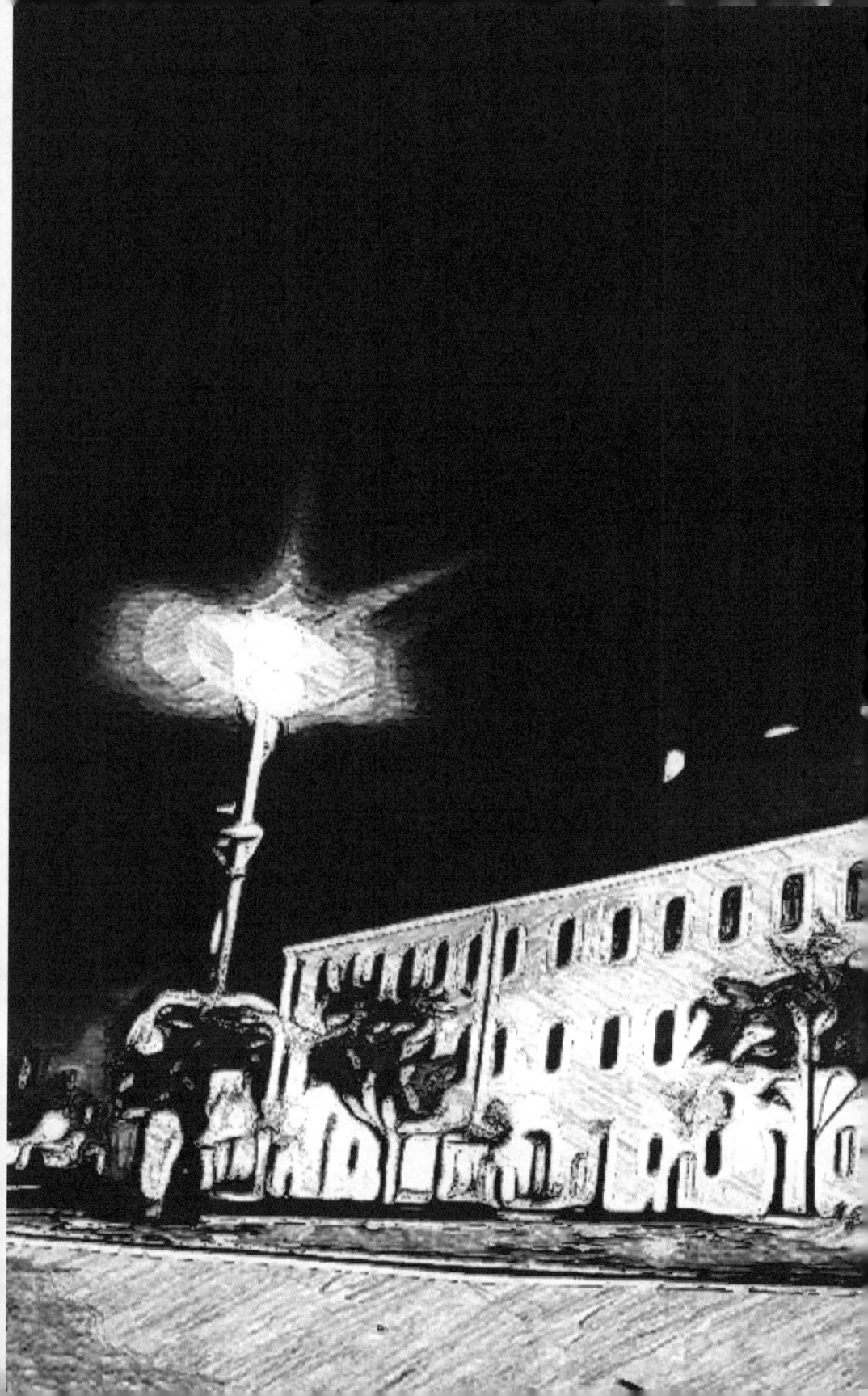

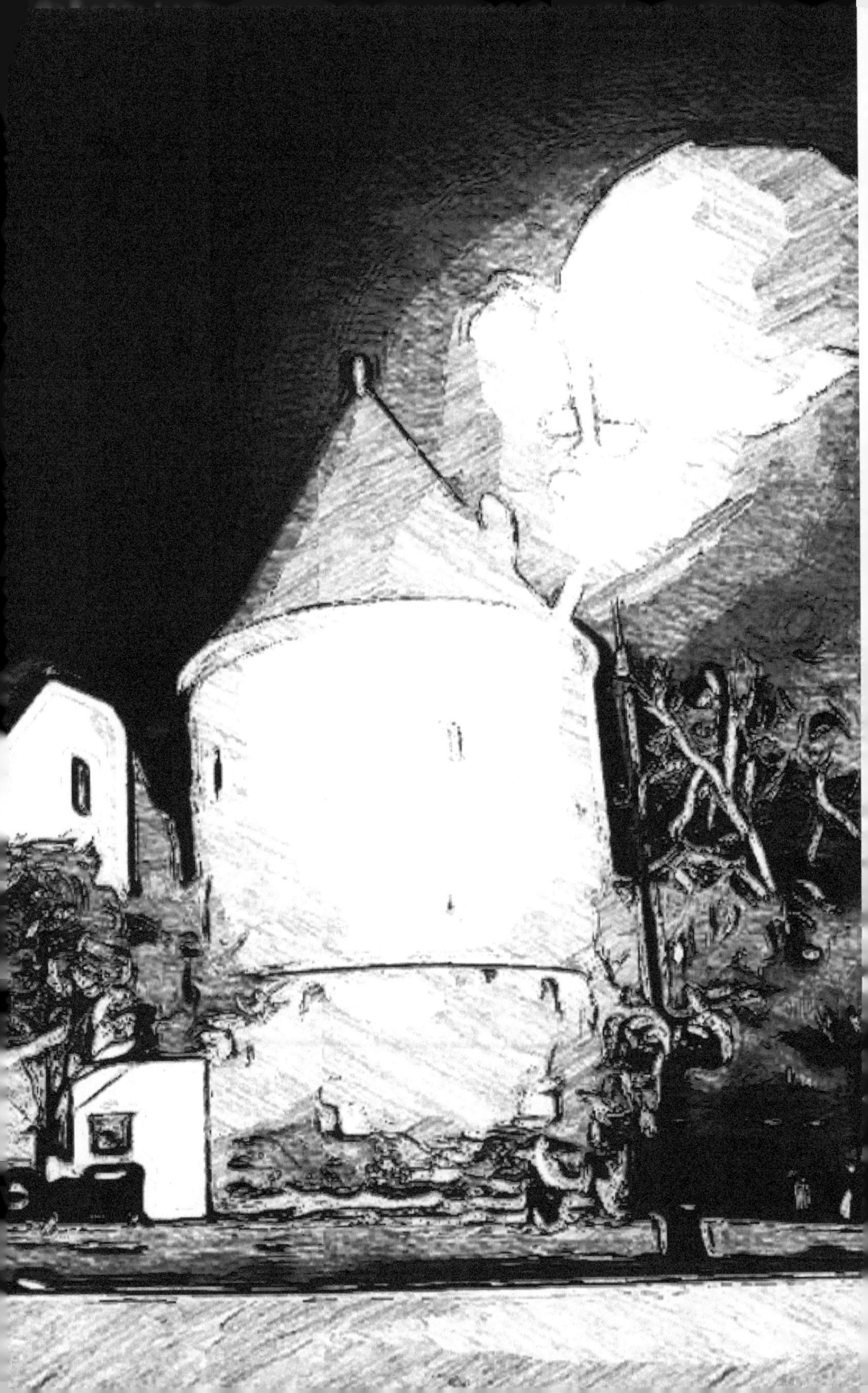

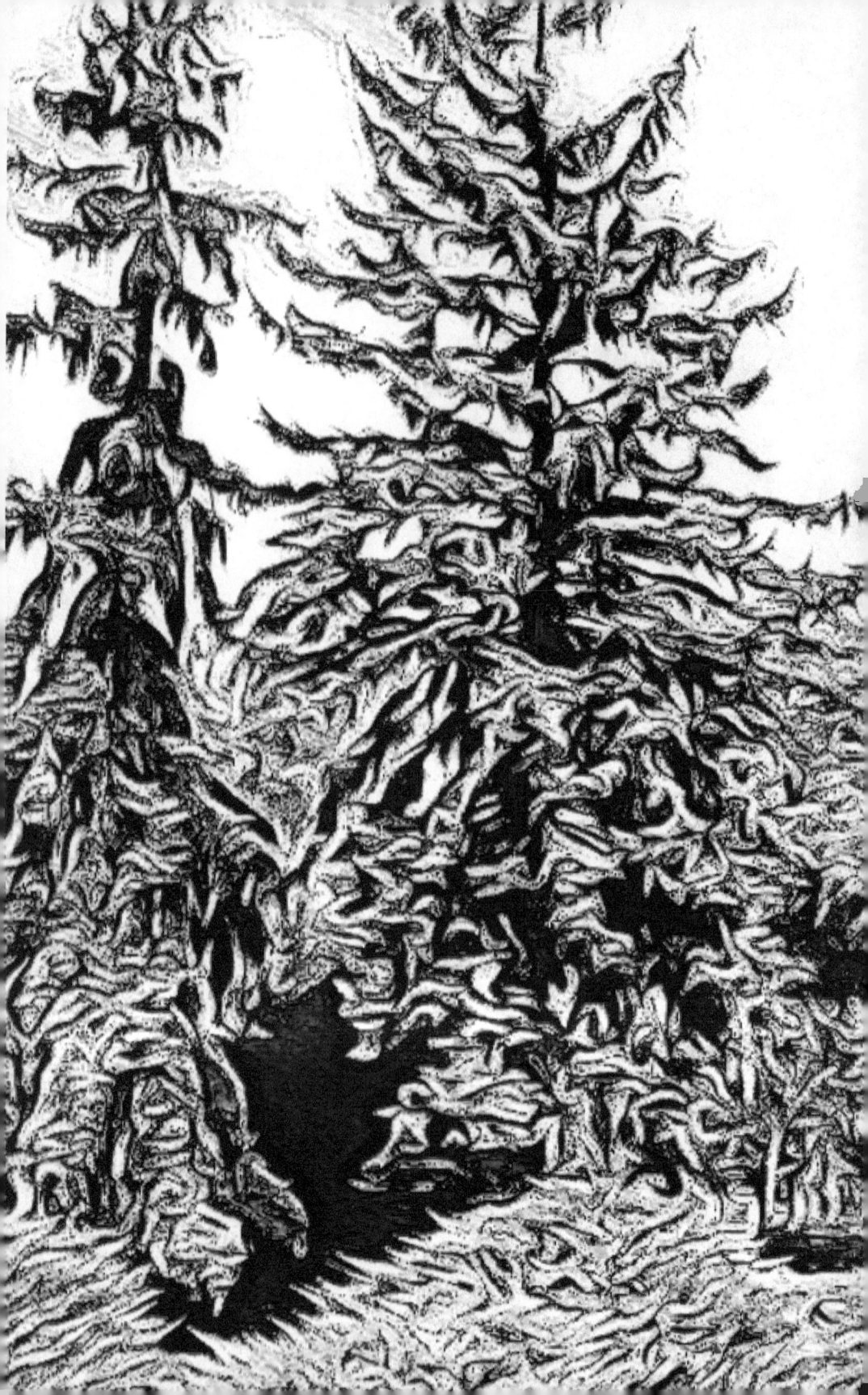

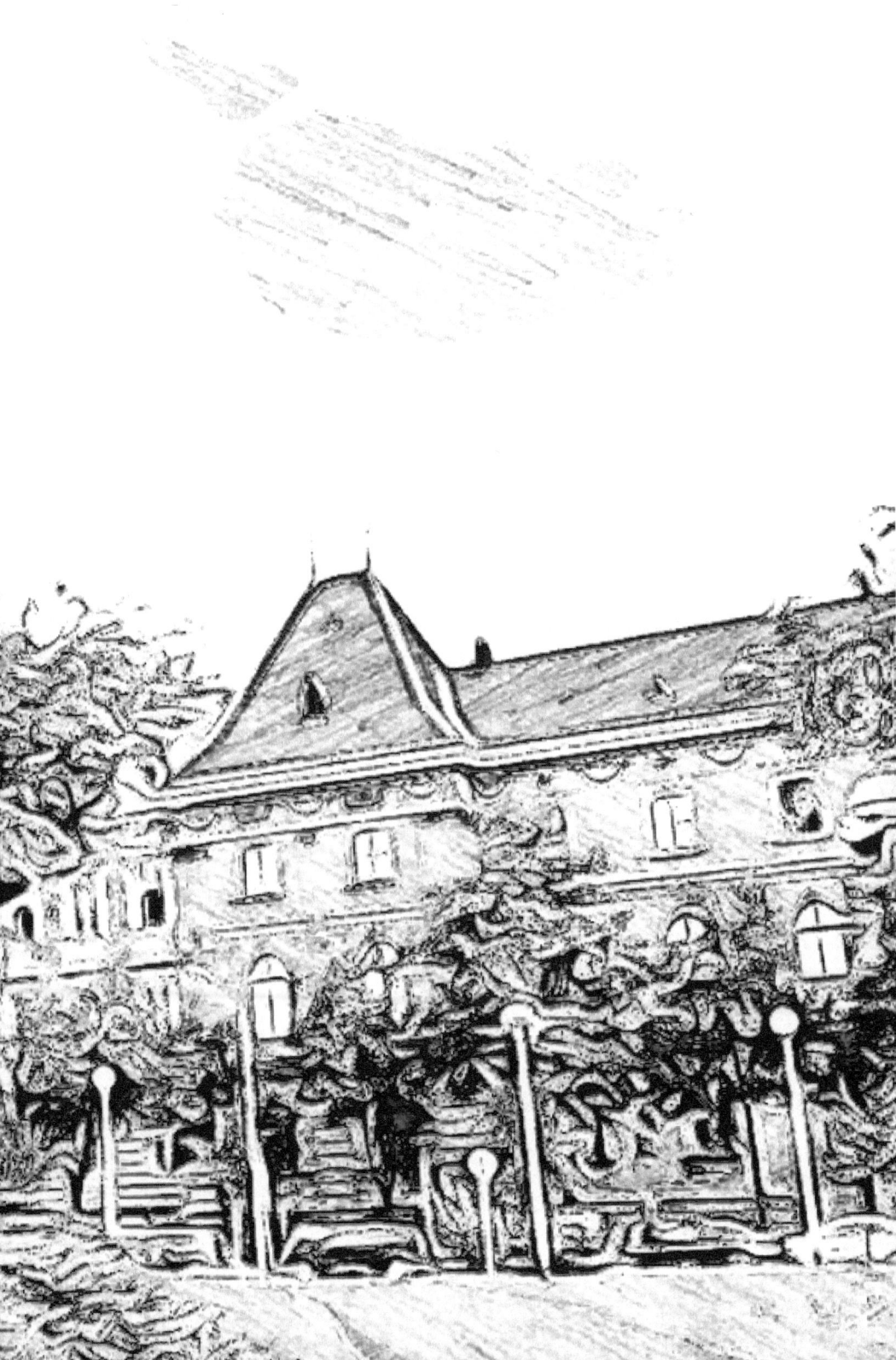

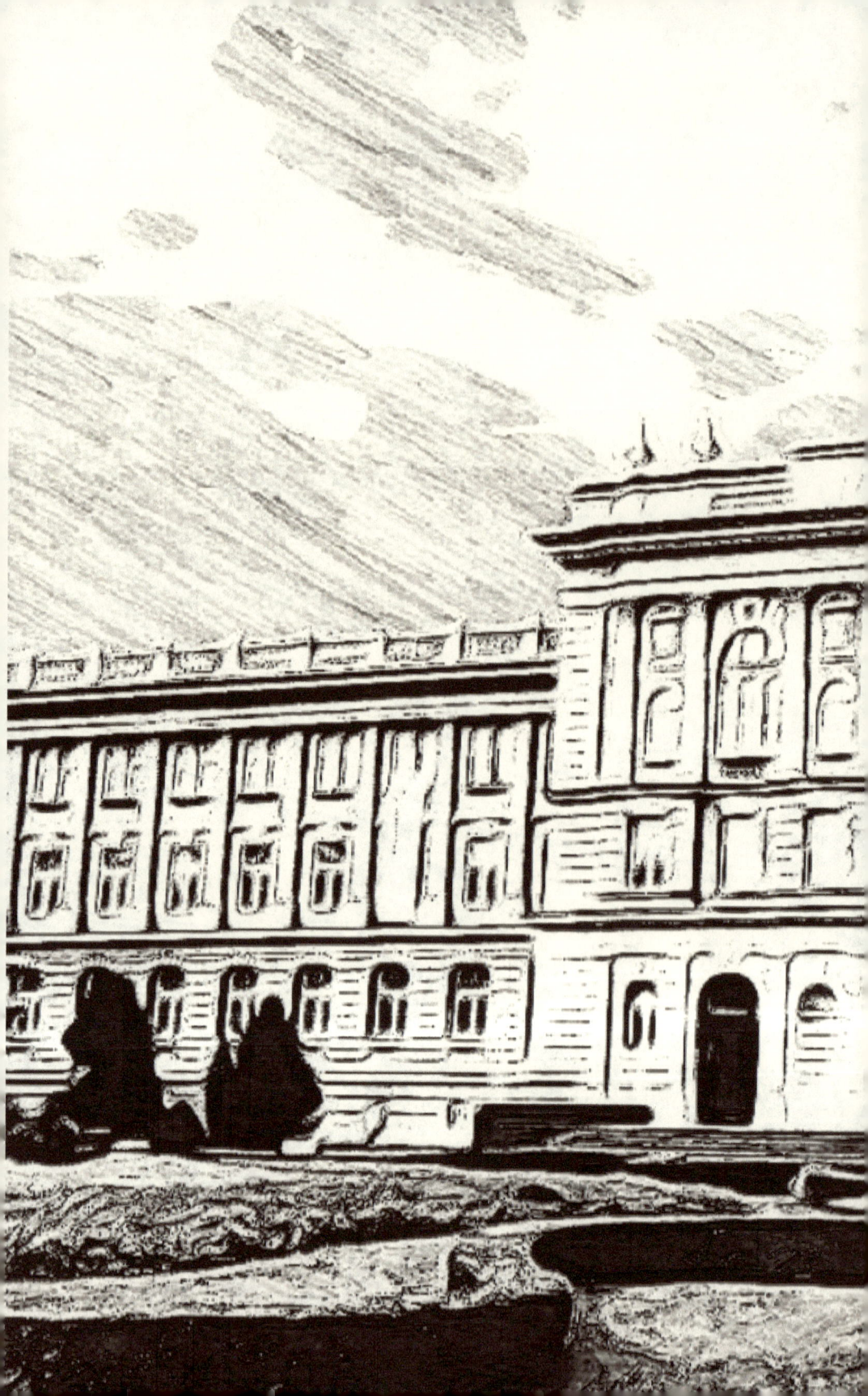

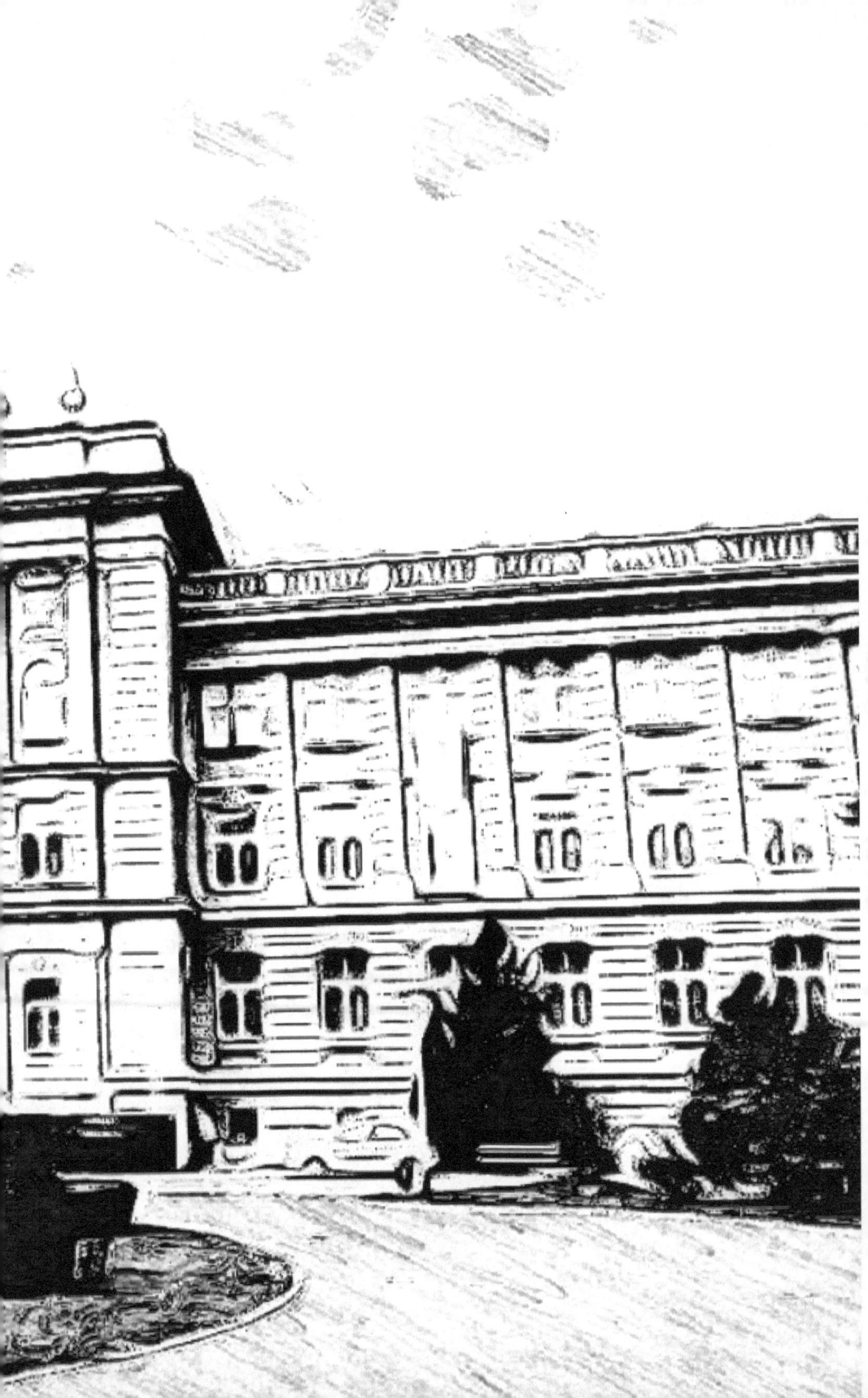

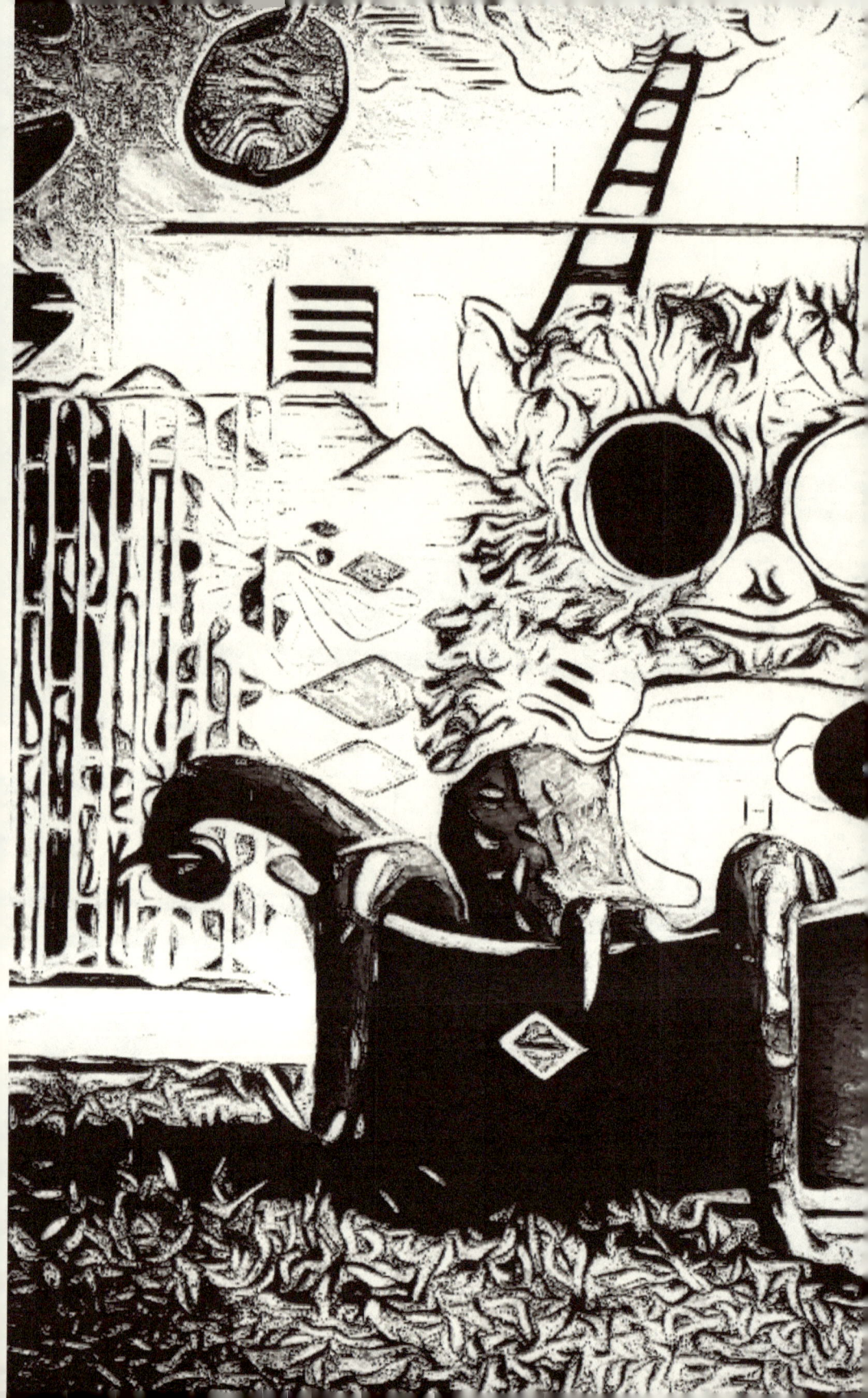

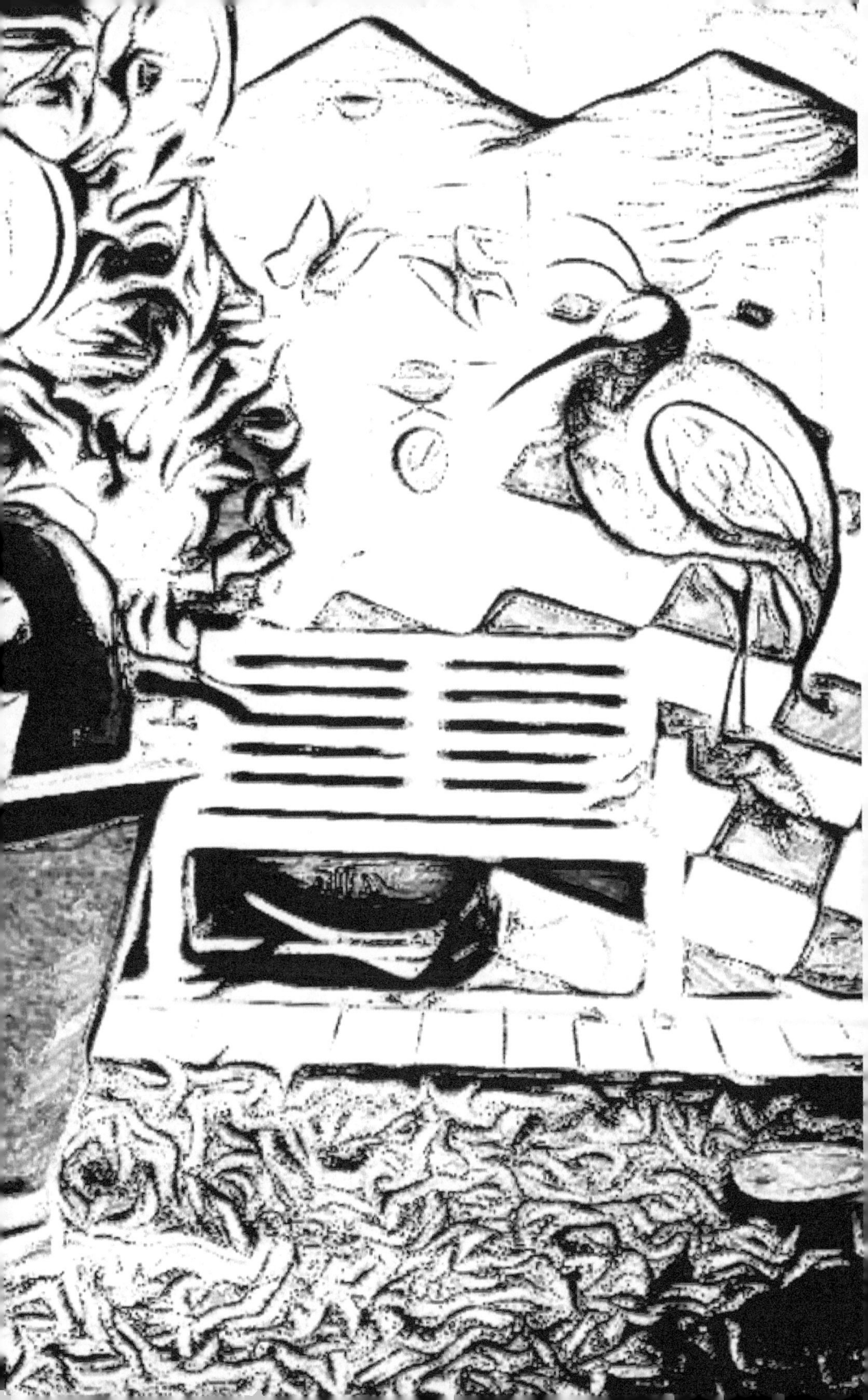

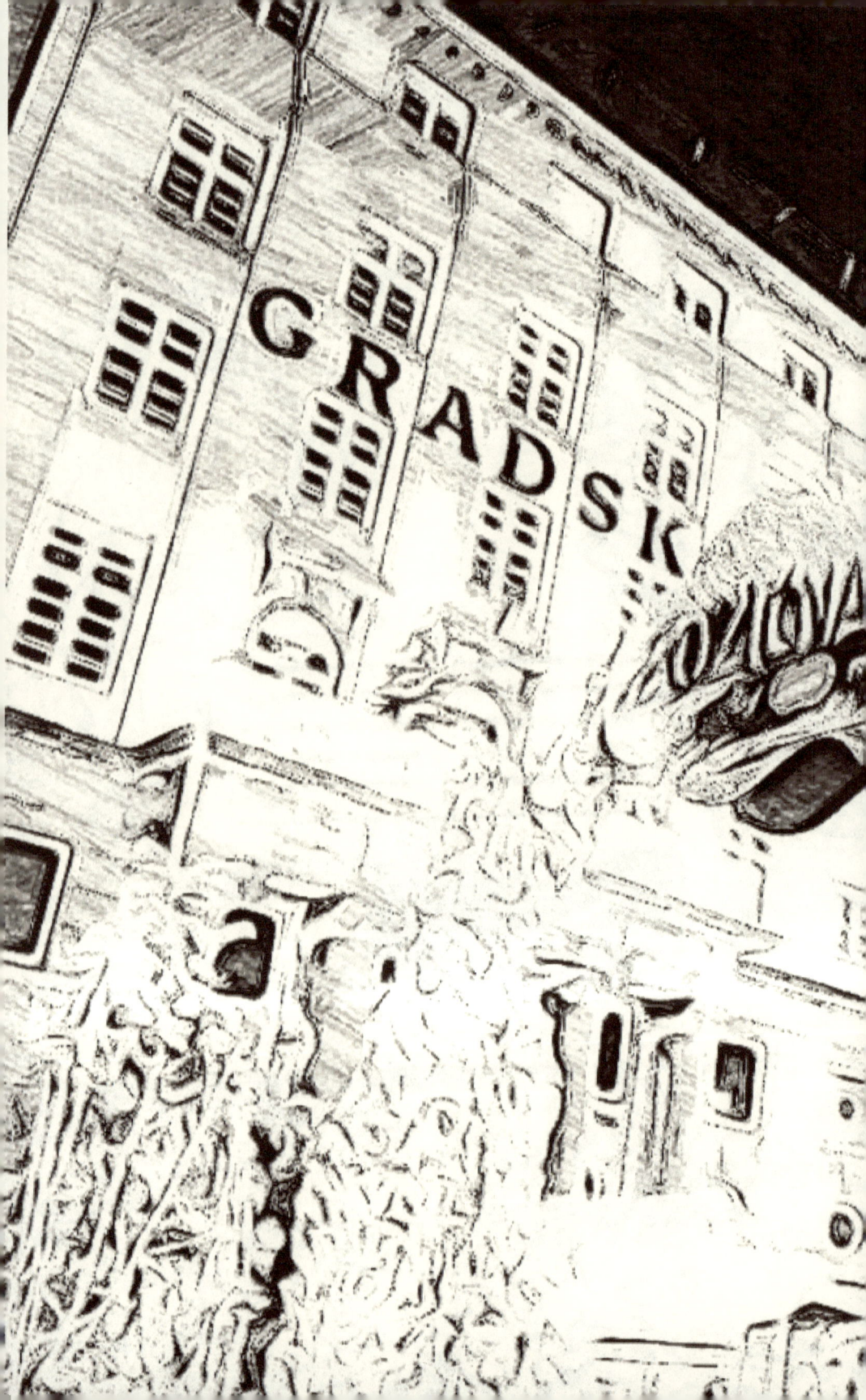

www.ingramcontent.com/pod-product-compliance
Lightning Source LLC
Chambersburg PA
CBHW021002180526
45163CB00005B/1865